The Black Arch

THE GOD
COMPLEX

By Paul Driscoll

Published January 2017 by Obverse Books
Cover Design © Cody Schell
Text © Paul Driscoll, 2017

Range Editor: Philip Purser-Hallard

Paul would like to thank:

*Dr Larry Kreitzer, who first showed me how to apply theology to the
medium of popular science fiction.
All those theologians who have considered questions of faith in
relation to Doctor Who, especially Andrew Crome, James McGrath,
Mark Goodacre, Caroline Symcox and Matt Rawle.
Jon Arnold for his insightful comments and encouragement.
Philip Purser-Hallard for his editorial expertise and patience.
Declan May, Stuart Douglas and Michael East for giving me the
faith and confidence to keep on writing.*

Also available

The Black Archive #1: Rose by Jon Arnold

The Black Archive #2: The Massacre by James Cooray Smith

The Black Archive #3: The Ambassadors of Death by LM Myles

The Black Archive #4: Dark Water / Death in Heaven by Philip Purser-Hallard

The Black Archive #5: Image of the Fendahl by Simon Bucher-Jones

The Black Archive #6: Ghost Light by Jonathan Dennis

The Black Archive #7: The Mind Robber by Andrew Hickey

The Black Archive #8: Black Orchid by Ian Millsted

Coming soon

The Black Archive #10: Scream of the Shalka by Jon Arnold

The Black Archive #11: The Evil of the Daleks by Simon Guerrier

The Black Archive #12: Pyramids of Mars by Kate Orman

The Black Archive #13: Human Nature / The Family of Blood by Naomi Jacobs and Philip Purser-Hallard

The Black Archive #14: The Daleks' Master Plan by Alan Stevens

Dedicated to the six wonders of my world, Daniel, Becci, Oliver, Hannah, Sophie and Luke.

CONTENTS

OVERVIEW

Serial Title: *The God Complex*

Writer: Toby Whithouse

Director: Nick Hurran

Original UK Transmission Date: 17 September 2011

Running Time: 47m 52s

UK Viewing Figures: 6.7 million

Regular Cast: Matt Smith (The Doctor), Karen Gillan (Amy Pond), Arthur Darvill (Rory)

Recurring Cast: Caitlyn Blackwood (Amelia Pond)

Guest Cast: Sarah Quintrell (Lucy Hayward), Amara Karan (Rita), Dimitri Leonidas (Howie Spragg), Daniel Pirie (Joe Buchanan), David Walliams (Gibbis), Dafydd Emyr (PE Teacher), Spencer Wilding (The Creature), Rashid Karapiet (Rita's Father), Roger Ennals (Gorilla)

Antagonists: The Creature

Responses:

'I'm feeling the rapture. That's because *The God Complex* by Toby Whithouse is one of the best **Doctor Who** stories ever.'

[Graham Kibble-White, *Doctor Who Magazine* #440]

'By adopting a surreal tone to the episode, it did help camouflage the fact that the plot made very little sense and apart from the scene where the hotel illusion rolled back and the monster died there was not much concrete in the way of real explanation of what was going on.'

[Gavin Fuller, *The Telegraph*, 17 September 2011]

SYNOPSIS

In an apparently perfect alien replica of a 1980s hotel, **the Doctor**, **Amy** and **Rory** encounter a disparate group of abductees: **Rita**, a young doctor; **Howie**, a teenage blogger; and **Gibbis** whose home, 'the most invaded planet in the galaxy,' has a culture of self-preservation through abject surrender.

They have been plucked from their everyday lives and set down in the shifting labyrinthine corridors of the hotel, where nightmares lurk in every room and previous guests' photos, captioned with their worst fears, adorn the lobby. This environment has sent the fourth member of the party, a gambler named **Joe**, insane. Apparently cured of his own fear of ventriloquists' dummies, he rapturously awaits his forthcoming consumption by **the Creature** that is the hotel's permanent resident. Joe has been tied up for his own safety, but he escapes to be killed by the lumbering Creature, leaving his body intact.

As the abductees discover their own rooms — Howie's containing girls laughing at his stammer, Rita's her overcritical father, Gibbis's a pair of Weeping Angels — they begin, like Joe, to exhibit an intermittent madness in which they are tempted to worship the Creature. The diary of **Lucy**, a police officer and previous victim, confirms the progress of this insanity. The Doctor transmits the voice of Howie, whose madness is furthest advanced, over the hotel's piped-music system to lure the Creature into a trap. It resembles a minotaur, and from its bellows the Doctor learns that it has been imprisoned here for so long it yearns for death. However, it escapes to kill Howie, who Gibbis has freed in the hope that this will satisfy the Creature.

After Rita, of whom the Doctor has become fond, is also taken, he realises that the Creature feeds on faith – Joe's trust in luck, Howie's in conspiracy theories, Rita's in Islam – but only once this has been converted to the worship of the Creature itself. As Amy, who found her own room earlier, begins to succumb, the Doctor realises that her faith in himself has made her vulnerable. They flee to Amy's room, where **Amelia**, her younger self, awaits the Doctor forever in a symbol of the abandonment she fears. The Doctor tells Amy that he has endangered her through his pride and vanity, and that he cannot save her now. The blow to her faith denies the Creature sustenance, and it begins to die.

The illusory hotel vanishes, revealing the spacegoing prison built by the culture whose god the Creature once was, to imprison and sustain it after their secular revolution. The Creature's final bellows describe the Doctor as akin to itself, and suggest that he, too, should welcome his forthcoming death[1]. Believing that what he told Amy is true, and to protect her from sharing his fate, the Doctor presents her and Rory with a house where they can live safely, and says goodbye.

---

[1] Seen in *The Impossible Astronaut* (2011).

THE MINOTAUR AND HIS MAZE

Throughout its history, **Doctor Who** writers have turned to stories and characters from Greek mythology for inspiration. These classic, often archetypical tales of gods, heroes and monsters have been appropriated in different ways. Some are etiological, investigating the origins of myths: *The Myth Makers* (1965) for instance, presents a fictional account of the history behind the legend of the Trojan Horse. Others, such as *The Horns Of Nimon* (1979-80) and *Underworld* (1978), recontextualise the myths into tales about alien cultures. The most common approach however, is far less explicit: myths are used as throwaway one-liners, borrowed lines, or subtle parallels which add little meaning to a story, but function as a nod to the initiated[2].

All storytelling is intertextual, insofar as we construct and interpret each new tale in the light of those we have already encountered (a similar mental process to facial recognition), and so when a writer alludes to a classic myth, it might even be accidental. Russell T Davies's *Last Of The Time Lords* (2007) was lauded by Christians and mocked by atheists in equal measure for portraying the 10th Doctor as a Christ-like figure[3]. It's all too easy to get carried away

---

[2] E.g. Pandora's box in *The Pandorica Opens* (2010).
[3] Russell T Davies denies making any deliberate Christological references to the Doctor (Davies and Benjamin Cook, *The Writer's Tale: The Final Chapter*, pp55-56). James Chapman argues such references reflect the prevalence of Christian allusions in Western culture (*Inside the TARDIS: The Worlds of Doctor Who – A Cultural History* (2006), p217). His view is unnecessarily Christocentric, since

with what biblical hermeneuticists call parallelomania[4], but like patterns in music, stories do have family resemblances. Joseph Campbell's influential book, *The Hero with a Thousand Faces* (1949) goes so far as to suggest a monomyth (the hero's journey) that can be used to link, say, Luke Skywalker to Gilgamesh, or the Doctor to Jesus. The shared mythical dimensions of a story are part of its genome, but the way we remember and learn is just as important. In a world that would otherwise be meaningless and chaotic, we make patterns, build associations and plot trajectories between unconnected events. **Doctor Who** fans are adept at highlighting influences behind a story, however tenuous or unlikely they might be. On one popular online forum, as each new episode is broadcast, a pinned section is included for such comments[5].

The God Complex (2011) started life as a basic brief from Steven Moffat: the nightmarish notion of our heroes being trapped in a labyrinthine hotel. Toby Whithouse's immediate response to this vaguest of ideas was to recall a favourite myth from his childhood: the Minotaur and his maze[6]. Not surprisingly, given that he was writing for a pre-watershed family show, Whithouse did not start with an examination of the existential and psychological meaning of the labyrinth. Instead his mind turned to the adventure stories of

---

the Jesus myth shares family resemblances with countless other hero stories.
[4] Sandmel, Samuel, 'Parallelomania', *Journal of Biblical Literature* 81, pp1-13.
[5] Gallifrey Base.
[6] Pixley, Andrew, 'The God Complex', *Doctor Who Magazine* (DWM) Special #31, p7.

old, looking for an example of someone being trapped and lost in a maze-like complex.

Whithouse's love of Greek mythology is well-known, but it is important to note that it stems not from an academic knowledge of the subject, but from his love of these stories as a child. He refers to them in the same breath as comics and horror stories[7]. That's not to say that deeper links to the tradition and history of the Minotaur myth are all accidental, or that he had not thoroughly researched the subject. As we shall see, the specifics of the story are such that the Minotaur functions not merely as the token monster of the week[8], but as the key to its interpretation. But this is a reminder that even though, perhaps more so than any of his **Doctor Who** contemporaries, Whithouse does not shy away from tackling those deeper existential questions, he is nonetheless consciously writing with the younger viewers in mind. As Robert Holmes said, 'If anyone decides that **Doctor Who** is an art form, its death knell will be sounded. It is good, clean, escapist hokum – which is no small thing to be.'[9]

Whithouse was no stranger to adapting Greek myths into new contexts and stories. His first play was a modern reimagining of the House of Atreus[10], and in his first contribution to the worlds of

---

[7] Cook, Benjamin, 'Favourite Worst Nightmare', DWM #439, p35.

[8] Graham Kibble-White notes how high-concept **Doctor Who** stories will often include an incidental monster, citing *The Doctor's Wife* (2011) (the Ood) and *Amy's Choice* (2010) (the Eknodines) (*The Essential Doctor Who* #5, p31). *Gridlock* (2007) (the Macra) is another example.

[9] Quoted in Gillat, Gary, *Doctor Who from A to Z* (1998), p77.

[10] *Jump Mr Malinoff, Jump*, 2010.

Doctor Who, the **Torchwood** episode *Greeks Bearing Gifts* (2006), the alien Mary manipulates Tosh by presenting herself as Philoctetes. The episode only briefly touches upon the myth, with Jack Harkness providing a rudimentary summary, but the parallels extend beyond Tosh's identification with the lonely, stranded hero[11]. Not surprisingly, the possibility of incorporating one of the most pervasive and inspiring of Greek myths into his third **Doctor Who** story were too good to refuse, despite the added complication that the Minotaur had already featured three times before in the show[12].

According to the legend, Pasiphaë the Cretan wife of King Minos gave birth to the Minotaur after sleeping with a bull that should have been sacrificed to the gods. The creature was subsequently imprisoned by Minos at the heart of a labyrinth. Each year (or seventh or ninth year), 14 Athenian youths would be sent to the labyrinth to be sacrificed to the Minotaur. One of them, Theseus, with the help of his lover, Minos's daughter Ariadne, killed the beast and ended the tribute[13]. The story has been thoroughly researched in the modern era, with its content being mined for historical, political and psychological significance. But its true legacy is to be found in the creative arts. Arguably, more than any other Greek myth, Theseus and the Minotaur has inspired generations of

---

[11] Amanda Potter, 'Beware of Geeks Appropriating Greeks' in Garner, Ross, et al, eds, *Impossible Worlds, Impossible Things* (2010).
[12] *The Mind Robber* (1968), *The Time Monster* (1972), *The Horns Of Nimon*.
[13] For a more detailed summary, see Garcia, Brittany, 'Minotaur'.

artists[14], dramatists[15] and writers[16] to use it as a lens through which to explore the tragedies and the triumphs of human existence. Emotive subjects abound, as basic fears and desires are brought to the fore. From the unnatural and forbidden love of Pasiphaë to the cruel abandonment of Ariadne by Theseus, and from the fear of the hybrid and the monstrous to the fear of falling at the last hurdle, the story takes its readers, viewers and hearers on an emotional rollercoaster. When told well, we the audience become participants, journeying into and out of the labyrinth and facing our own nightmares in the process.

There are three particular approaches to the story:

1. Those which focus on Theseus.
2. Those which focus on the labyrinth.
3. Those which focus on the Minotaur.

---

[14] See for instance Cassone Meister (1402-89), Sandro Botticelli (1445-1510), William Blake (1757-1827), George Frederick Watts (1817-1904), Pablo Picasso (1881-1973), Salvador Dali (1904-89), Richard Patterson (1963-).

[15] From Dante's *Inferno* and Shakespeare's *A Midsummer Night's Dream* to contemporary productions, such as David Harsent and Harrison Birtwhistle's *The Minotaur: A Libretto* (2008) and an acclaimed 2016 adaptation of the myth by the Unicorn Children's Theatre, London.

[16] See the discussion on Borges and Dürrenmatt below. For a contemporary treatment see Mark Z Danielewski's *House of Leaves* (2000), George Szirtes, 'Minotaur in the Metro', published in *Reel* (2014), and Carol Rumens's *De Chirico's Threads* (2010).

Other characters in the narrative such as Ariadne[17], Minos[18] and Daedalus the architect[19] occasionally take central stage, but they feature far more prominently in academic pieces than they do in works of art.

At its most basic level this is a story of a hero defeating a monster – whether the Minotaur, his own personal demons, or the Cretan king. Numerous films have followed this approach, sometimes even replacing Theseus with another protagonist such as Sinbad, Hercules or more recently Percy Jackson[20]. They tend to be dualistic battles between good and evil, with the Minotaur's monstrous form disguising the tragedy of its own situation. This mode of storytelling is adopted in *The Horns Of Nimon*, with Seth playing the role of Theseus:

DOCTOR

Poor old Seth.

ROMANA

Poor old Seth?

---

[17] E.g. 'Bacchus and Ariadne', Titian (1522-23).
[18] E.g. 'The Last Judgement', Michelangelo (1536-41), which depicts Minos as the judge of the underworld.
[19] Daedalus has his own continuing story, whereby he makes wings for himself and his son Icarus in an effort to escape the labyrinth within which he himself has been imprisoned by Minos. Works featuring the architect tend to focus on his son's fate, so for instance 'The Fall of Icarus', Rubens (1636).
[20] *Sinbad and the Minotaur* (2011), *Hercules in the Maze of the Minotaur* (1994), *Percy Jackson and the Olympians: The Lightning Thief* (2010).

DOCTOR

Yes. Well, just imagine the legends Teka's going to build up around him. He'll have to spend the rest of his life trying to live up to them. It's terrible.

ROMANA

I suppose that's how legends are made.

The God Complex has plenty to say about the Doctor's heroic status, but is Whithouse writing the story from the perspective of the Doctor being Theseus? Certainly, there are parallels to be drawn between the Doctor's abandonment of Amy and Rory at the end, and Theseus' rejection of Ariadne. In one version of the myth, Theseus' guilt at causing the death of his father is what leads him to leave Ariadne behind, choosing to protect her by ending the relationship. Earlier in the story, the Doctor has his aide, his own Ariadne, in the form of Rita (much to Amy's irritation). Whithouse wants the audience to make the assumption that this will be another example of the hero overcoming the beast and so the Theseus and the Minotaur analogies are useful devices. Our confidence in the Doctor sets up the reversal of fortune. We realise at the same time as he does, that he has seriously misjudged the situation, and since we have put our own faith in him, it hits us for six too.

Theseus as a character is far from unique. He is the archetypical hero who slays the beast, whether it be a dragon, lion, giant or other mythical creature. The feature that has always made this particular myth stand out from the crowd is the location of the Minotaur, at the centre of a labyrinth.

Traditionally a labyrinth is different from a maze, in that there is a single pathway to the centre. There are no dead ends or multiple routes, just a disorientating, winding pattern, in which the traveller gets lost, not because he needs a map to navigate his way through, but because once inside he cannot see the end or the beginning. Its pattern deceives the traveller enough to make him fear that he is on the wrong path, as it winds nearer and then further away from the centre. Ariadne's thread was not so much a tool for navigation as a source of reassurance.

In recent years, mazes and labyrinths have seen a resurgence in popularity. Perhaps a statement on our postmodern condition, they are not so much puzzles, but experiences of worship, pleasure or therapy. Works of art in themselves, they have also inspired numerous movies from *Cube* (1997) to *The Maze Runner* (2014).

Breaking the boundary between maze and labyrinth, the notion of reconfiguring walls adds to the illusion of being trapped. It makes the maze almost impossible to navigate, and the labyrinth potentially eternal. A long-standing feature of many video games, such as the **Monkey Island** series (1990-2009) and the *Doctor Who: Destiny of The Doctors* PC game (1997), it is a cruel and manipulative deception on the part of the designer, one that confounds our choices at every turn.

Given that the starting point for *The God Complex* was the concept of the hotel, we might have expected the story to focus on this aspect of the myth. Instead, one of the later additions to the script, the rooms within the hotel, becomes more important than the connecting corridors[21]. Steven Moffat perhaps finally fleshes out his initial brief in series nine's *Heaven Sent* (2015), with Whithouse's script moving in an altogether new direction.

The third major approach to the legend explores the nature of the Minotaur. It frequently becomes a metaphor for the self. Unsympathetic treatments consider it to be the instinctive beast within; the personification of those animal urges we seek to tame. The classic Greek writer Pausanias demythologises the creature, ironically observing, 'For even in our time women have given birth to far more extraordinary monsters than this.'[22] As Graham Sleight notes:

> '...it often makes sense to consider something monstrous as the personification of one human trait to the exclusion of all others, and so as a cautionary tale about the dangers of that trait.'[23]

In Dante's *Inferno* that single characteristic, embodied by the Minotaur, is unrestrained violence.

Sympathetic treatments of the beast focus on its innocence, imprisonment and wish to be free. Here the creature represents alienation and loneliness, born out of misunderstanding and a sense of not belonging. Borges' short story, 'The House Of Asterion' (1947), forces the reader to reassess the myth from the perspective

---

[21] Cook, Benjamin, 'The Nightmare Man', DWM #432, p22. Whithouse states they only appeared in the last two drafts, completely changing the tone of the piece.
[22] Pausanias, *Description of Greece*, 1.24.1.
[23] Sleight, Graham, *The Doctor's Monsters* (2012), p1.

of the Minotaur. As Martin Tilney describes it, Borges' approach allows 'the reader to connect directly to Asterion's psyche and experience the world through his consciousness.'[24]

The labyrinth in this version is not a prison, but it is paradoxically infinite in size and number of rooms, and though the beast finds a way out, he quickly returns inside because of a mutual fear between him and the outsiders. This brief story tells of the creature's desire for redemption, his longing to be released from the labyrinth and of how that can only come through his death. He gets his wish within the text when in the final line Borges abruptly shifts to the third person, introducing Theseus and Ariadne into the story:

> 'The morning sun reverberated from the bronze sword. There was no longer even a vestige of blood. "Would you believe it, Ariadne?" said Theseus. "The Minotaur scarcely defended himself."'[25]

At this point, the reader's perspective changes from mirroring the fear and disgust of the Cretans, to realising that the creature has been misunderstood, misrepresented and mistreated. The redemption of the Minotaur is completed by the reader.

A more extended favourable treatment of the Minotaur is by Swiss author Frederick Dürrenmatt, in his illustrated poem, *Il Minatauro* (1985). Like Whithouse, Durrenmatt was drawn to the story as a

---

[24] Tilney, Martin, 'Waiting for Redemption in the House of Asterion', p55.

[25] Borges, Jorge Luis, 'The House of Asterion', trans James E Irby, in Borges, *Labyrinths: Selected Stories and Other Writings*, p172.

child. But it had a far more profound effect on the young Swiss, leading to a recurrent nightmare in which he saw himself as the Minotaur, trapped in the labyrinth with murderers lining up outside to slay him. The nightmare-inducing myth reinforced his own sense of isolation after his family moved to the city of Bern. Feeling socially and physically set apart, he started seeing labyrinths all around him, externalising his own lostness. In later life his writing shifted from a focus on the labyrinth to the Minotaur itself, culminating in *Il Minatauro*[26]. In the ballad, the beast's maze is constructed of mirrors; wherever he looks, he sees himself. His deliverance comes when Theseus arrives disguised as the Minotaur. Thinking that he has finally found a companion, the Minotaur is killed.

Originally Dürrenmatt was commissioned to write an opera, but this failed to materialise. However, recently the character has been brought to life on the stage, inspired by Dürrenmatt's poem[27]. As the co-director Stephen Langridge sees it:

> 'What makes this piece special is that the Minotaur is the subject of his own drama, rather than simply being the object of everyone else's fears [...] he's a victim, but a victim who then becomes a perpetrator of violence.'[28]

Midway between the sympathetic and unsympathetic perspectives, as both the monstrous and the misunderstood, the perpetuator

---

[26] Ziolkowski, Theodore, 'Dürrenmatt's Fiction'.
[27] Harsent and Birtwhistle, *The Minotaur*.
[28] Ivan Hewett, 'The Minotaur: Father and Son Venture into the Labyrinth', *The Telegraph*.

and the victim of violence, the Minotaur has been characterised as a creature who embodies the conflicting nature of human desire. His hybrid nature fascinated the artist Picasso, who recognised his own contradictions in the beast. Perhaps the most discussed of all his treatments of the Minotaur is 'Minotauromachy' (1935). The creature in *The God Complex* physically resembles Picasso's drawing more than it does the Nimon.

Whithouse's Minotaur falls on the sympathetic side of the spectrum, and it is this aspect of the myth that, thematically, takes centre stage in *The God Complex*. As he explained at a Comic-Con convention: 'You have to find the humanity, sympathy of it. [...] There's nothing more boring than a straightforward villain who just wants to do evil.'[29]

Like Borges' Asterion, the creature is longing for redemption, yearning for death, and like Durrenmatt's Minotauro it is surrounded by mirrored surfaces. For much of the episode the Minotaur is difficult to pin down and we are only given enticing glimpses into its nature, as translated through the Doctor. The Doctor's initial reaction to the creature is to marvel at its beauty, seeing beyond the stereotypical labels and giving it the benefit of the doubt. This non-judgmental trait has been a consistent feature of the character down the years.

Monsters come in all shapes and guises, but it is not always appropriate to label them as evil. There are those who are destructive or harmful because of their inherent nature; they have

---

[29] Nededog, Jethro, 'Comic-Con 2011 Meets **Doctor Who**'s Matt Smith'.

no capacity to be anything other[30]. This is how the Doctor initially sees the Minotaur: 'You have lived so long even your name is lost. You want this to stop. Because you are just instinct. Then tell me. Tell me how to fight you.'

Sleight makes the helpful distinction between: A, creatures with the capacity of speech who can be reasoned with, and B, those who are elemental threats[31]. So is the Doctor's attempt to communicate a pointless exercise? Is he trying to make a type B monster into a type A monster? The tragedy of the Minotaur is that its imprisonment has taken away any free will it might once have possessed, and its isolation has driven it to the point of madness. It has moved from type A to type B because of its environment. The Doctor struggles at first to interpret the creature, because like the hotel itself, the Minotaur no longer makes sense. At this point the Doctor has not worked out the reason for the creature's imprisonment and he assumes that the hotel itself, or its architect, is the villain of the piece. The Doctor's reasoning, were he to have articulated it, might have gone something like this: *perhaps in its natural habitat, feeding off of the fears of others would have released them instead of killing them.* The Doctor's god complex is shown in his belief that not only can he save the Minotaur's victims, he can also save the prisoner.

Most sympathetic versions of the Minotaur are autobiographical in nature, but here Whithouse's point of comparison is not himself. Nor is it the viewers, or the universal struggle between love and

---

[30] See Sleight, *The Doctor's Monsters*, p199.
[31] Sleight, *The Doctor's Monsters*, p199.

instinct. Instead, the Minotaur represents the Doctor. The point is made explicit in the stand-out line of the story, as once again the Doctor articulates the Minotaur's thoughts.

> '"An ancient creature, drenched in the blood of the innocent, drifting in space through an endless, shifting maze. For such a creature, death would be a gift." Then accept it, and sleep well. "I wasn't talking about myself."'

This final twist in the story is cleverly foreshadowed throughout the episode, both visually and conceptually. Early on, the Doctor stands under a set of horns whilst eating an apple, and later we see his reflection superimposed onto the Minotaur as he hunts the creature. Whilst the creature parallels its world to the Doctor's playground, of all of time and space, the prison itself shares striking characteristics with the TARDIS. They confound spatial dimensions and whereas once the two ships could alter their appearance, they are both stuck on an Earth-based desktop theme.

The main conceptual link between hero and beast is spelt out in the episode's title, *The God Complex*. In a twist on the classical myth, the creature is revealed to have been part of an alien race who roamed the universe looking for planets and peoples to subjugate by setting themselves up as their gods. Whithouse no doubt was inspired by *The Horns of Nimon*, which follows a similar theme (albeit one slightly more faithful to the original tale), and so quite naturally the two races are presented here as distant relatives[32].

---

[32] Toby Whithouse, on why he did not simply make the Minotaur a Nimon, tells *Starburst Magazine* that aside from the possible rights issues, the fact that the Nimon were not the most popular of

22

The Doctor, by seeing the Minotaur as a mirror of himself, is forced to reconsider his need and use of travelling companions, a theme that runs through all of Whithouse's episodes. Consequentially, the adventure becomes a pivotal point in the series' arc, as the events trigger the Doctor letting go of Amy and Rory.

Within the **Doctor Who** universe, the Minotaur has featured on two other occasions, plus a throwaway line in *The Creature from the Pit* (1979), in which the Doctor suggests he supplied Theseus with the thread. In *The Mind Robber* (1968), the beast makes a cameo appearance as one of a number of fear-inducing mythical creatures. It is defeated by the Doctor asserting that the creature is a projection, as he encourages Zoe to repeat with him 'the Minotaur is a mythical beast. It doesn't exist.'[33] Whereas in *The God Complex*, the ship reverts to its uncloaked form, in *The Mind Robber*, where the setting is the main threat, the Minotaur and other creatures are the ones to give way. The beast is there to elicit fear instead of faith.

The next appearance comes in the Jon Pertwee adventure *The Time Monster* (1973), where the creature is real, but transposed into the myth of Atlantis. Still in the heart of a maze, he functions as a guard instead of a prisoner. The agile third Doctor physically defeats the creature to recover the Crystal of Kronos. In both stories the Minotaur plays a bit part and the ancient legend is part of a wider complex of borrowed myths.

Doctor Who enemies was a factor (Southall, JR, 'Interview: **Being Human** Showrunner Toby Whithouse').
[33] *The Mind Robber* episode 3.

In discussing the role of myth in **Doctor Who**, David Layton observes that the most common approach is for writers to borrow from known stories (both ancient and modern), retelling them in a new setting. He is quite dismissive in his assessment of such stories: 'Whatever imaginative or psychological power the myths themselves may have had [...] becomes only spectacle.' This may be a legitimate criticism of *Nimon* for instance, but does *The God Complex* buck the trend?

Of all the **Doctor Who** stories to have mined the Minotaur myth, *The God Complex* is the most explicit. The creature is called 'Mr Minotaur', a nickname coined by the Doctor. Upon perusing the database, the monster fits the description so well that the Doctor answers Amy's question, 'what is it? A minotaur or an alien? Or a minotaur alien?' with 'It's both actually.' But not only does it take some of its cues from the original Cretan tale, it finds inspiration from a diverse range of modern and postmodern treatments by deliberately focusing on the beast itself and by using it as a mirror with which to reinterpret the Doctor. In connecting the ancient myth, not with an alien race, who remain mysterious and whose background is irrelevant, but with the Doctor, the most familiar character whose journey the viewer will continue to share, the story is definitely 'work[ing] with myth on a deeper, archetypal level.'[34]

---

[34] Layton, David, *The Humanism of Doctor Who*, p102.

THE MINISTRY OF LOVE

Whithouse's induction into the inner circle of go-to **Doctor Who** writers was more surprising than most, particularly as his first commission was to bring back the iconic characters of Sarah Jane Smith and K-9, so beloved by then producer Russell T Davies[35]. Whilst the likes of Davies, Paul Cornell, Mark Gattis, Steven Moffat and Gareth Roberts had been creatively involved in continuing the myth during the so-called 'wilderness years', Whithouse's fan credentials were untested. He describes himself as a fan, having grown up with Tom Baker as his Doctor, but concedes that when he first met with the other writers to discuss the revived series, he was overwhelmed by their superior knowledge of **Doctor Who** mythology[36]. Although now well known for his genre-based work, Whithouse received his first commission for series two (2006) before the pilot for **Being Human** (2008-13) aired. His credentials were brief but impressive, with the actor-turned-writer having devised the Channel 4 series, **No Angels** (2004-06). Whithouse has since established himself as a regular writer and has contributed five stories to date.

In some ways Whithouse approaches the show like any other, starting with a basic concept, before meticulously fleshing out the characters. Only then do the stories and set pieces begin to take shape[37]. He highlights his own style of working by comparing himself to Steven Moffat who tends to go straight to script. By the

---

[35] *School Reunion* (2006).
[36] See his comments in 'Script Doctors.'
[37] 'Toby Whithouse: BBC Writersroom Interviews **Being Human** Writer and Creator'.

time Whithouse sets about writing the dialogue, he has already completed numerous draft outlines[38]. Not surprisingly, Whithouse's work has become known for its focus on characters. He goes so far as to suggest that the genre exists to highlight everyday human themes and situations[39].

Despite bringing his tried and tested character-based approach to **Doctor Who**, Whithouse has adapted his writing style, stepping out of his comfort zone to tackle new genres. Of all his scripts to date, *The God Complex* best showcases his strengths and sees him writing on familiar territory. However, Whithouse admits to having struggled with the unique demands of writing for the show. After finding his feet, he has settled on a formula that is immediately apparent in his scripts: 'the Doctor has to arrive in a certain place, assess the situation, and he has to make a decision, quick, and that's probably going to be the wrong decision.'[40]

Earlier on in his **Doctor Who** career, Whithouse conceded that there are certain unique techniques he adopts when writing for the show, not because of its genre, so much as its pre-watershed target audience:

> 'All of the slow progressions of character and storyline and so on are thrown out of the window [...] you need lots of big moments, big conflicts every couple of scenes. [...] That was something I learnt from Russell [...] And actually, that simplifies the process, because your task is then to get

---

[38] Arnopp, Jason, 'Ghost Writer', DWM #492.
[39] 'Adaddinsane', 'Toby Whithouse Q & A: A Report'.
[40] Cook, 'The Nightmare Man', p24.

yourself to the next big explosion or the next chase down a corridor.'[41]

The early drafts of *The God Complex* were nonetheless initially conservative compared to the final script, and Whithouse was tasked with adding more 'big moments' to his story[42]. With the Minotaur a sympathetic character who spends much of the time in the shadows, and with the location deliberately drab and claustrophobic, the adventure lacked sufficient spectacle. Whithouse needed to delve deeper into his characters in order to ensure that they remained the focus of the piece, otherwise those high-octane set pieces he now had to incorporate would gratuitously detract from the initial concept[43]. Cleverly he found a conceit that would enable his characters to be even more distinctive, one that would at the same time pepper the story with an array of colourful and creative scenarios: the nightmare rooms.

George Orwell's dystopian novel, *Nineteen Eighty-Four* (1949, hereafter *1984*), has become as ingrained in popular imagination and culture as the ancient Minotaur myth. Like the Cretan legend, elements within the narrative have taken on an independent life of their own, most notably Big Brother, Room 101, and newspeak. Although quite possibly mediated through his knowledge and enthusiasm for the work of comic book writer Alan Moore,

---

[41] 'Script Doctors.'

[42] Cook, Benjamin 'The God Complex', DWM #438, p24.

[43] Arguably, the weakness of Russell T Davies's set-piece approach was the occasional use of action pieces purely for the sake of spectacle, such as the Robot Santas and spinning Christmas trees of *The Christmas Invasion* (2005).

Whithouse's nightmare rooms are clearly inspired by the 1949 novel[44].

Towards the end of the book, Winston Smith is tied to a chair and tortured in Room 101, by being confronted with his worst fear: rats; a multivalent symbol for human depravity, disease and poverty. It is the last resort of the Ministry of Love in their efforts to strip him of all independent and critical thought. The aim of the psychological and physical torture is to induce not merely a condition of obedience to the ruling elite, but an absolute love for Big Brother. The state wins and Winston ends up dead to himself, his body an empty shell, with the capacity for free thinking lost in total surrender to the state: 'He had won the victory over himself. He loved Big Brother.'[45] By the end of the novel, Winston Smith wants to die and dreams his own physical death. In *The God Complex*, Rita's fate is sealed by exactly the same desire as she surrenders in unconditional love to the Minotaur, resisting the Doctor's intervention whilst knowing that she is going to her death: 'I'm not frightened. I'm blessed, Doctor. I'm at peace.'

Rita is not protecting the others by asking them to stay away. She is ensuring that no outside force can shatter the illusion of her death as a victory or prevent her from becoming a non-person. Her faith, once centred around her culture, has been redirected towards the god as power, who breaks all memory or connection to the past. It

---

[44] Whithouse cites Moore, the author of the Orwell-inspired *V for Vendetta*, among his most influential authors (alongside David Manet and PJ Hammond) (Martin, William, '10 Things we Learned from **Doctor Who** Writer Toby Whithouse's Twitter Q & A').
[45] Orwell, George, *Nineteen Eighty-Four* (1949), p342.

is the intended fate of everyone drawn to the prison. Death at the hands of the Minotaur is not simply the ending of a life, it is the stripping of a worldview, rendering meaningless the cultural and social elements that lie behind that philosophy as well as the choices of career and lifestyle that have been lived on the back of it. The creature doesn't simply feed on different faiths, it converts its victims first.

Rita's death, and the Doctor's sense of responsibility for it, are unique. Many have died in the crossfire of his interventions, for the greater good; and a few notable companions and associates have even become martyrs for the cause, facing death with defiance, such as Adric and Harriet Jones[46]. But Rita and the others in the complex are killed because of his mistake. Their death has no value and resolves nothing. The Doctor questions the Minotaur as to whether or not it is waiting for its prisoners to be ripe. The tragedy of the story is that he speeds up the process for Rita by encouraging her to turn to faith.

What is lacking in the telling of the story is any context behind the events. The depressing dystopian vision of *1984* helps to provide a bigger picture in which to ground the otherwise out-of-time-and-space prison. The allusions to *1984*, as with the Theseus and the Minotaur story, add levels of interpretation over and above those offered by the story itself. They encourage the knowledgeable viewer to fill in the numerous gaps in the narrative, in a controlled yet liberating way, insofar as they inform conjecture with intertextual analysis. But without recourse to such frames of

---

[46] *Earthshock* (1982), *The Stolen Earth* (2008).

reference, *The God Complex* suffers from the charge of being lightweight in terms of plotting[47]. The story requires a level of investment beyond the enjoyment of escapist entertainment, otherwise its unanswered questions might sully its reputation.

1984 is not a straightforward analogy, because the situation is abnormal for the Minotaur. It has been isolated from its people and driven to madness over centuries of captivity. All we are told about the Minotaur's race is that they travelled from planet to planet, looking for people to subjugate; looking for worshippers. The prison is thus *1984* after the revolution. We are not told who it was that rose up against the minotaurs or indeed what happened to the rest of them, but the creature's captivity demonstrates that they turned the tables on their oppressors; somehow their consciousness was reawakened.

The Doctor has always stood up for the oppressed, removing the obstacles that mute or deter protest. Time and time again he empowers individuals and civilisations by exposing the lies that had brought compliancy through deference and by countering the threats that had brought compliancy through fear. But on this occasion the Doctor has arrived after the event; the revolution has already taken place, and yet he is surprisingly casual about it. 'They descend on planets and set themselves up as gods to be worshipped. Which is fine, until the inhabitants get all secular and advanced enough to build bonkers prisons.' The ship is not the first highly advanced vehicle for administering justice to have crossed

---

[47] See for instance Fuller, Gavin, '**Doctor Who** *The God Complex*: BBC One Review', and Risley, Matt, '**Doctor Who** *The God Complex*: Review'.

the Doctor's path in series six (2011)[48], but it is by far the cruellest. The Minotaur has been trapped inside it for so long that he describes it as an endless hell. It is the creature's hell and not Rita's Jahannam. The beast is kept perpetually alive through the ship's ability to detect new sources of faith. The choices of who to bring on board are the ship's and not his. Alone and without a wider audience to play to (since the ship extracts individuals not societies), or fellow predators he can share the spoils with, there is no satisfaction in what limited power he retains. The torturer has become the tortured. The sacrifices of others serve merely to prolong the Minotaur's miserable existence, providing no material reward, in contrast to the ruling elite's luxurious lifestyle in *1984*, a life that he once presumably had before his captivity and isolation.

This is the only time 11th Doctor ever uses the word 'bonkers', indicating that he has borrowed it from Rita, whose preventable death still haunts him. But it is a flippant word in the circumstances. Neither the injustice of the Minotaur's original intentions, or the taking of victims by the ship solely in order to torment the creature with its eternal loneliness, seems to have angered the Doctor[49]. His earlier fit of rage is self-directed, an example of the very god complex that Rita perceptively pointed out to him just minutes earlier. Either the builders of the prison are callous enough to be unconcerned about the slaughter of innocents

---

[48] The Teselecta (*Let's Kill Hitler*, 2011).

[49] A line that was edited out makes the Doctor seem even less concerned about the injustices behind the prison and the Minotaurs' oppression of other cultures: 'Maybe he was a good god to them… maybe this was his pension' (Pixley, 'The God Complex', p16).

required to keep their prisoner in perpetual suffering, or they have become like their former oppressors, criminalising faith, history and imagination. Either way, the totalitarianism of the ruling elite in *1984*, and the psychological techniques they employ to obliterate diversity and freedom of thought, are mirrored in the episode.

The *1984* analogies are not limited to the nightmare rooms. The ship is peppered with security cameras, calling to mind the 'Big Brother is watching you' meme. But in this instance, who is doing the watching? Certainly not the Minotaur, but nor can it be the creators of the prison. It is all part of the automated illusion of the ship's design. Unless the ship is sentient, and nothing in the script warrants such a conclusion, then etiologically, the cameras exist for added authenticity. As such they are no more significant in purpose than the carpets, the other room furnishings or even the *Look-In* magazine. But for both the writer and director, they are extremely convenient tools for telling and showing the story. So is there a deeper, symbolic meaning behind them, or are they just useful devices for scripting and directorial concerns? Is their prominence alongside the Orwellian nightmare rooms merely a coincidence?

Plucked from different times and spaces into a hotel with shifting rooms and corridors, the inhabitants of *The God Complex* would be hopelessly lost without the CCTV system. Tellingly however, it is only the Doctor who catches on to this potential weakness in the ship. He becomes the omniscient one by locating the operating heart of the system. His intervention finally gives meaning and purpose to the cameras. It does not make him the Big Brother figure in the literal sense, but it neatly riffs on the idea that he is governed by a god complex. The absence of a sentient Big Brother means that the roles are played vicariously; partly by the Minotaur but ironically also by the victims of the unmanned and unnamed regime. It is no coincidence, therefore, that the party have tied one of their own to a chair even before the Doctor, Rory and Amy have arrived on the scene. It's a deeply cynical reading of the role that even the oppressed play in propping up the system. Without the political and social commentary and context, what we are left with is an internalisation and individualisation of an oppressive system, reducing it to a morality tale.

In *1984*, the nursery rhyme 'Oranges and Lemons' plays an important role. It is gradually remembered by Winston as the story unfolds and charts the degree of his deconditioning. Reminded of long-forgotten cultural symbols, he becomes fixated on recovering the whole rhyme. Winston treats each recovered verse as a personal triumph in his quest to break free of the system. But his tragic fate is foreshadowed and made inevitable by the shocking twist in the last lines of the song: 'Here comes a candle to light you to bed. Here comes the chopper to chop off your head. Chip chop, chip chop, the last man is dead.' It is a bleak warning that enlightenment will bring about his destruction[50].

The rhyme as a harbinger of death is another element of *1984* woven into *The God Complex*[51]. Gambler Joe quotes from the

---

[50] See Orwell, *Nineteen Eighty-Four* 112-14, 168, 206. Note too the book's working title – 'The Last Man in Europe'. Perhaps reflecting Orwell's isolation on Jura whilst writing the novel, the title (rejected by the publisher) may also be a nod to the 'the last man is dead' line.
[51] The rhyme is a favourite of Whithouse's, also appearing in **Being Human**.

33

rhyme as he nears death and pledges allegiance to the Minotaur. On one level, it is a reminder of the faith of the gambler, with the symbols of oranges and lemons strongly associated with slot machines. Just as the addition of the last two lines (not found in the earliest versions of the ditty) interrupt the flow and kill the rhyming game dead, so too Joe's faith is about to be converted into edible adoration for the Minotaur. But the song carries an additional layer of meaning because of its association with *1984*. More obscure than the Room 101 and camera references, it is precisely because of its obliqueness that the rhyme alerts the viewer to the interpretative possibilities of Orwell's book in understanding the story. It suggests that the other *1984* references are not just nods to popular, watered-down versions of Room 101 and Big Brother, but have something of deeper value to present[52].

Following a well-trodden **Doctor Who** plot device, *The God Complex* is a story of individuals being picked off one by one[53]. Within the story therefore, the nursery rhyme acts as a premonition, foreshadowing the unavoidable demise of the characters, including Joe who somewhat psychotically recites the penultimate line. But the spectre of death has loomed over the whole season, with the Doctor apparently resigned to his fate at Lake Silencio. A standout feature of Moffat's tenure as executive producer is the use of rhymes to add gravitas and an air of

---

[52] The same can be said for the reference to 'The Pasiphaë Spa' in relation to the Cretan Minotaur mythology.
[53] C.f. *The Robots of Death* (1977), *Horror Of Fang Rock* (1977), *Mummy On The Orient Express* (2014) and *Under The Lake / Before the Flood* (2015) to name but a few.

foreboding to individual stories[54], or to frame them within the wider arc of a series. 'Tick tock, goes the clock...' features either side of *The God Complex*, with *Closing Time* introducing a new verse to the poem from *Night Terrors* (both 2011), using it to reveal River Song as the impossible astronaut who will assassinate the Doctor. The newly-penned rhyme shares a family resemblance to the traditional 'Oranges and Lemons', and both function to unsettle the viewer and shake our confidence in the Doctor. Although Joe stops short of reciting the final line of 'Oranges and Lemons', the implications of 'the last man is dead' will particularly resonate with viewers who have followed the whole series and are all too aware that the Doctor's next death will, supposedly, be his last[55].

In *1984*, the 'Oranges and Lemons' rhyme is itself spoilt by the machinations of the masters of doublespeak. It should be a symbol of resistance, a throwback to a forgotten past, and a sign that all is not lost. But it turns into a symbol of submission, a surrender to the horrors of the present, and a sign that all hope is futile. References in popular culture to the rhyme as used in *1984*, sometimes focus on the positive aspect of resistance[56], but *The God Complex* homes

---

[54] E.g. *The Beast Below* (2010), *A Good Man Goes To War* (2011). The fact that these feel like nursery rhymes in their meter and style, whilst perhaps a reflection on the increased role of children during Moffat's tenure, also adds an uncanny and sinister quality, reminiscent of the girl in *Remembrance of the Daleks* (1988).

[55] From the trauma of his execution as already played out in *The Impossible Astronaut* (2011). After the events of *The Day Of The Doctor* and *The Time Of The Doctor* (both 2013), it makes sense to retcon the Doctor's own fear that he is on his last regeneration into *The God Complex*.

[56] E.g. the video game *Half-Life 2*.

in on the ironic twist to foreshadow its own tragic ending. Even the Doctor's apparent gift of freedom to Amy and Rory, the ease in which it is accomplished and the ostentatiousness of it all, comes across as the last desperate act of a man with a god complex. He makes no allowances for the past horrors the couple have been through together, and he is extraordinarily naïve to believe in a fairytale ending for Rory and Amy. It is doomed to end in failure, as we discover in the minisode series *Pond Life* (2012).

The Doctor is also at his most fatalistic around this time, seemingly content to accept injustices and the unnatural order of things. At the heart of the comedy Ood in *Pond Life* is a deeply troubling contrast. Rory and Amy are uncomfortable with the Ood's slavish subservience to them, but the Doctor tells them to relax, because that's the way he is meant to be. Even though, and perhaps partly because, he manages to escape his physical death, something has been lost, and like Winston Smith, the Doctor has stopped resisting. Significantly, in the next story after *The God Complex*, the saviour figure is the Doctor's friend, Craig Owens. Even whilst no longer travelling with anyone, for fear of consequence, he still has to depend on others. The 'Oranges and Lemons' line and the wider *1984* references in *The God Complex* foreshadow a long and dark period for the Doctor. He might have cheated death with the Teselecta, but in the next series he will soon become the forgotten.

A SHINING EXAMPLE

Standing directly between the mythical and supernatural Minotaur strand, and the psychological and political *1984* strand, Stanley Kubrick's 1980 adaptation of Stephen King's *The Shining* (1977) is the third major influence behind *The God Complex*. The film tells the story of struggling writer Jack Torrance's descent into madness inside the mysterious and haunted Overlook Hotel. Jack becomes the live-in caretaker of the isolated hotel, moving in with his wife and psychically gifted son Danny. Danny's visions and voices are channelled by his imaginary friend, Tony, 'the little boy who lives in Danny's mouth'. Danny is able to see physical representations of ghosts and demons that haunt his father.

One of the more plausible interpretations of *The Shining* covered in the documentary movie, *Room 237* (2012), is that the movie is a reworking of the Theseus and the Minotaur myth. At the end of the film Jack dies inside a hedge maze, a location that Kubrick added to King's novel. The association of Jack with the Minotaur is foreshadowed elsewhere in the movie: there are moments when Jack appears taurine-like – as if he's a bull about to charge; there is a poster of a skier who looks like the Minotaur beside another of a cowboy riding a bull; and in another scene, Jack's wife, Wendy, makes a comment about leaving a trail of breadcrumbs, reminiscent of Ariadne's thread. *The God Complex* is far more explicit in its mining of the Minotaur myth, but its association with *The Shining* extends far beyond this shared mythical inspiration.

The seminal film sets the stylistic tone of *The God Complex*, with both pieces deliberately provoking questions about what is real. Together, Whithouse and director Nick Hurran capitalise on the themes, location and techniques used in the movie to ensure that the story falls firmly in the horror genre. At the time, Kubrick's work was atypical of horror-movie conventions, but the genre has branched out largely because of his influential work, and his techniques are often repeated, in combination with more staple horror elements. The horror elements in *The God Complex* are not solely derived from *The Shining* (Hitchcock's influence is also noticeable in parts), but the links with Kubrick's film are explicit.

The ship's hotel form calls to mind the Overlook Hotel with its numbered nightmare rooms. Both 'hotels' resist any attempts to escape them. They have been deliberately created to entrap and break their occupants by triggering primal fears and psychological trauma. The usual rules of time and space do not apply, giving them an air of transcendence and sentience. And just in case the viewer thinks it might still be coincidental, both the Doctor and later Rita note that the hotel looks like something from the 1980s.

Aside from the obvious similarities in setting, a number of thematic links are also made. The automatic writing of Lucy ('Praise him') links to Jack's typewriter ('All work and no play makes Jack a dull boy'), which like Joe's bonds and the muzak operates with no apparent human agency. That the Doctor is comparable to Jack, both through similarity and dissimilarity, is made clear by the way the two characters are repeatedly seen through mirrored surfaces[57]. They are both driven to a point of uncontrollable rage (for quite different reasons and with quite different outcomes). The

---

[57] The Doctor's face is reflected in the reception bell, the cassette player, water, and multiple mirrors.

two characters are forced to respond to the futility of their work and their lack of success (Jack as a writer and the Doctor as a saviour figure). Jack's and the Doctor's lifestyles and psychological state present risk to their closest allies.

There is also a clear association between young Amy and Danny, who both talk to 'imaginary' friends. The pre-credits introductory sequence which accompanied all the episodes of the season, including *The God Complex*, on international broadcast (and is now used for the same purpose on Netflix), ends with Amy narrating her story of how she met the Doctor, with flashbacks to young Amy. Unlike Danny's Tony, her friend is real; at least in a physical sense. The Doctor is not a means of accounting for her powers. However, the hero figure she imagines him to be, is no more real than Tony. Even more incidental images, such as the photographs on the wall[58] and the man in a gorilla suit, call to mind iconic moments from the 1980 film[59]. The contrast between Danny's ESP and the non-working telephones is individualised in *The God Complex*, with the Doctor successfully interpreting the grunts of the Minotaur, yet unable to reach Rita on the telephone.

Whilst the list of parallels is extensive, the most significant contribution of *The Shining* is in the way in which the story is told, rather than its subject matter or meaning. The unreliability of both narratives generates a correspondingly unsettling effect, even if the

---

[58] Displaying characters who have died in the respective hotels.
[59] C.f. The man in a bear suit in *The Shining*, despite its more adult themes and associations.

stories and themes are quite distinct[60]. Unusual camera angles[61], jump cuts, breaks in logic, and the steadycam which follows a character's movement through the corridors are all shared techniques. In this respect the links to *The Shining* are primarily concerned with the viewers' responses and engagements with the story. It has things to say about how we both participate in and interpret the action[62].

Ironically, one of the characters in *The God Complex* represents a certain type of respondent to *The Shining*. Because of its open-endedness, numerous theories as to the movie's meaning have been proposed according to the interpreters' worldview and

---

[60] *The Shining* uses psychology as misdirection, admits Kubrick, 'to forestall the realization that the supernatural events are actually happening' (Ciment, Michel, 'Kubrick on *The Shining*'). *The God Complex* misdirects the viewer into expecting this to be a run-of-the-mill base-under-siege story, with the Doctor playing detective. (note the allusion to **Sherlock** (2010-) with the jump-cuts to the Doctor spotting clues on Joe).

[61] Such as above or below the eye level of the subject. See for instance the trike scene in *The Shining*, with the camera on the floor level, below Danny, giving an air of surrealism to the scene (Pramaggiore, Maria, and Tom Wallis, *Film: A Critical Introduction* (2005), p110). In *The God Complex*, the opening shot of Lucy is with the camera positioned on the floor, and this perspective is repeated throughout the episode. The shots looking down the spiralling staircase, and then alternating from a position above to below the Doctor, Rory and Amy on the stairwell, allow the viewers to experience the environment's disorientating effect with the characters.

[62] Re the participatory effect of the steadycam see Pramaggiore and Wallis, *Film*, p119.

beliefs. Howie types, the conspirator theorists, argue that the number 237 alludes to Kubrick having faked the moon landing[63]. Howie's presence in *The God Complex* reminds the viewers that the story cannot be pinned down by one reading at the expense of all others and alerts us to the fact that a priori beliefs shape interpretation[64]. Whithouse, like Kubrick, deliberately leaves some fundamental questions unanswered, from individual details such as the content of the Doctor's room, to bigger plot issues such as who built the ship in the first place. The fact that Howie doubles as the unfortunately stereotypical geek makes him a cipher for the most engaged and invested viewers. His particular faith in conspiracies, which requires reading between the lines, is one that Whithouse has observed in the fanbase of which he himself is a part[65]. Certainly, endless theories about specific details of an episode have been proposed, sometimes to the detriment of the episode itself.

There is a clear link between the mind of the conspiracy theorists and the tendency of passionate fans to over-interpret small, incidental details. A good example arising from *The God Complex* was the ongoing speculation that at some point in the series the Doctor had been switched with a 'ganger', the artificial duplicates from *The Rebel Flesh / The Almost People* (2011). Many fans noted

---

[63] *Room 237.*
[64] These extreme prescriptive conspiracy theory readings have a suitable air of madness about them. See Glieberman, Owen, 'Room 237'.
[65] 'I absolutely love the passion and speculation of the fans. If I'm honest sometimes I have a little giggle when you all scuttle off down a blind alley' (Keogh, Garrett, 'Toby Whithouse Answers Your Questions: Part 3').

at the time that the Doctor liking the apple and solving the Rubik's cube were such overt breaks in continuity, that they could only be clues that the man on screen is an imposter. So, whilst allowing for a degree of provisionality and creativity in interpretation, certain limits are called for. Those limits are set by the way in which the viewer experiences the story. The techniques, borrowed from *The Shining*, encourage the viewer to participate in the drama emotionally and not watch it from a critical distance, looking for clues or faults. Consequentially, it is one of those rare **Doctor Who** stories that is deeply affective at a personal level. For every fan speculating and theorising about the content of the Doctor's room, 20 more viewers were asking themselves what would have been behind their door.

Kubrick's version of King's novel paints a far bleaker picture of human existence, and his characters are unsympathetic[66]. The horror of the piece moves away from external, supernatural forces towards the monstrous within, before returning to the supernatural at the denouement, with the tantalising prospect of Jack's reincarnation into the past. The location, like the ghosts, becomes a metaphor for Jack's state of mind. At first the long, empty corridors convey the meaninglessness of his life[67], that sense of boredom and of going nowhere that triggers his breakdown, and then as the hotel becomes more and more surreal and disorientating, the viewer is left to feel increasingly claustrophobic despite its vastness. It's a claustrophobia born from not being able

---

[66] Jameson, Richard, 'Kubrick's *Shining*'.

[67] Danny's trike ride is a good example (see Jameson, 'Kubrick's *Shining*').

to see the way out, rather than from the tightness of the space. The rooms and even their fixtures and fittings teasingly suggest portals through which to escape, but they are always unobtainable or frustratingly lead to other portals[68]. Mirrors feature heavily in the film, suggesting an infinite regression, one that always leads back to Jack[69]. The viewer is left feeling trapped by Jack's spiralling descent into madness.

The whole tale is filmed from the perspective of the characters involved in the drama and this vantage point, rather than any exposition and explanation that might enable us to empathise with the characters, is all that we have to draw us into their story. Jack's self-obsession effectively turns the other residents into ghosts: their stories do not intertwine; it's as if they are all existing in a parallel universe. We have no choice but to become part of his nightmare, whether we chose to side with him or his victims. It's certainly not 'horror' in the traditional sense, and that makes it all the more unsettling. The Overlook Hotel is for the most part brightly lit, almost mocking the viewer's lack of enlightenment. The expectations of the genre are repeatedly confounded, so that whilst there are the occasional scary set pieces, we are revolted rather than terrorised.

The God Complex uses its setting as a metaphor for the Doctor's wanderings across time and space. As Amy explains in the international intro sequence, she is running with him constantly. In the prison, they are going round in circles, frequently ending up in

---

[68] Byrne, Joseph, 'Mise-En-Scene in Stanley Kubrick's *The Shining*'.
[69] Jameson, 'Kubrick's *Shining*'.

the same corridor. Dialogue is limited and backstories sparse, so that viewer empathy has to be based predominantly on visual clues as we are drawn into the minds of the hunted. There are lights everywhere and yet frequently the viewer is left in the dark.

Every point of correspondence in style, setting or structure also serves to illustrate the divergences between the two stories:

1. *The God Complex* is not about the Doctor's family battling alone against the isolating and disorientating effects of the prison and ultimately against each other. If anything, Rory and Amy are pulled closer together.

2. Unlike Jack, the Doctor finds redemption, to a point.

3. The supporting characters are not ghosts, whether literal or metaphorically subservient to a story that does not concern them. They have their own backgrounds, and just enough information is provided in the script, within the limits of the page count, to create sympathy, especially for Rita. It is repeatedly stated that certain nightmares are not intended for the current occupants of the ship, giving a sense that the Doctor, Rory and Amy are in no way unique.

4. The hell of the ship is the Minotaur's and not the Doctor's[70].

---

[70] At the most immediate level, there is of course a symbolic equivalence between the Minotaur's situation and the Doctor's, one that is unpacked throughout this study. The Doctor as we shall see does indeed come face to face with his own nightmares, but this is not quite the same as being his hell. The Doctor will encounter that personal hell in *Heaven Sent* – a place of total isolation, with nobody to save except himself.

The God Complex could have been written in such a way as to make the story solely about the TARDIS crew. Rita and the others could have already been processed, their pictures already part of the trophy wall. It could have depicted the Doctor as the tormented hell-bringer who has to save Amy and Rory from himself, but Whithouse stops short of completely demonising the hero. He is flawed, his motivations analogous but not identical to the Minotaur's. Even when he is breaking Amy's faith in him, he is far gentler than the seventh Doctor in his belittling of Ace in *The Curse of Fenric* (1989). He is an amenable character with a god complex – as if that makes it better[71]. And the favourable comparison with the Minotaur uncomfortably overlooks the creature's past abuses on account of its pitiful state in the present. The Doctor is shown to be like the Minotaur, but only by Whithouse first presenting the creature as a victim.

Hurran's exquisite directing makes use of many of Kubrick's techniques, but for the most part the point of view is not primarily that of the characters, but of the prison itself through the lens of its own cameras[72].

At significant junctures in the story however, Hurran does switch the point of view to a character, thereby stressing its importance, most notably during the possession scenes and when the Doctor sees Amy morph in and out of her younger self. This subjective approach to showing the story makes the cameras function like

---

[71] Our assumption of the Doctor's goodness is triggered very early on, when Amy is shocked by Rory describing the trio as 'nice'.

[72] See Sandifer, Phil, 'A Great, Great Partnership (The God Complex)'.

unreliable narrators, forcing the viewer to question the reality of what they see. Temporal and spatial anomalies, such as the splicing of the possession scenes, add to the hyperrealism, and suitably convey the shifting nature of the labyrinth from Steven Moffat's original brief.

Like *The Shining*, the episode places the viewer into the heart of its world, leaving them unnerved, confused and disturbed. But it does so at a relentless pace, lacking time for any of Kubrick's trademark slow, real-time scenes. Whithouse has said that one of the best pieces of advice he'd received as a new writer, was to enter a scene as late as possible and leave it as early as possible[73]. We can clearly see this at work in *The God Complex* from the opening scene. There is little time to breathe in this relentlessly paced story, which is problematic given the dramatic shift towards the end in the Doctor's self-understanding and his relationship with Amy and Rory.

Once the illusion of the hotel is broken down, and reality is restored, the script and direction return to an orthodox mode of storytelling. The viewer can be confident that from the moment the ship morphs into its natural state, we can trust the narrative, even if our faith in the Doctor has been shaken. We expect to now find out what has really been going on, and to be allowed to empathise with the characters because the rules of our engagement have changed: we should be moving away from the Kubrick subjectivism to a more traditional involvement as sympathetic onlookers. As

---

[73] 'Toby Whithouse: BBC Writersroom Interviews **Being Human** Writer and Creator'.

with Dorothy, back in Kansas, the extraordinary should have become ordinary again, our characters brought back from this surreal land of make-believe to their real lives (even if in their case this includes travelling across time and space in a dimensionally transcendental blue box). The viewers experience a sense of relief because of the modal shift, as if we have escaped from the labyrinth too. But it quickly becomes apparent that this is no 'as you were' moment. The Doctor does not undo his faith-stealing words to Amy after the death of the Minotaur; we suddenly jump to the Doctor dropping Amy and Rory off. The potential emotion behind the farewell scene is underplayed and makes no reference to the story that preceded it, leaving some disgruntled viewers to feel that it was tagged onto the back of the story because of continuity requirements. Others expressed the opposite opinion, bemoaning the fact that from their perspective the story was just a protracted way of signalling the departure of Amy and Rory.

Their farewell is foreshadowed in the story at several points. Even before the Doctor has been confronted with his god complex, he has already joked about replacing Amy with Rita[74]. Rory, sore from the events of *The Girl Who Waited* (2011), is at his most cynical when he warns with utmost seriousness disguised as humour, 'Every time the Doctor gets pally with someone, I have this overwhelming urge to notify their next of kin.' Rory is fleetingly offered a way out from the labyrinth. Since the significance of faith

---

[74] By using Alan Sugar's phrase 'you're fired' (**The Apprentice**), the Doctor is deliberately associating himself with the entrepreneur who, for the purposes of the cameras at least, revels in his assumed power to control the destiny of others.

has yet to be revealed, it initially casts doubt in the viewers minds about his level of commitment, suggesting he has mixed feelings about continuing to travel with the Doctor. Amy's opening rant about not seeing the incredibly tall people, shows that unlike her husband, she still has a thirst for adventure. Later, when reading back Rory's lack of faith as the reason for the fire exits appearing, and having seen the Doctor tear Amy's faith to shreds, the viewer knows that a farewell is being teased.

The story then marks a significant turning point: without it, the Ponds would still be travelling with the Doctor. But in that final scene, apart from an echo of Rita in Amy's final line, 'he's saving us,' the dramatic events in the prison go without comment. Immediately before the cut to the town house, Gibbis is asking for a lift home. We can only presume he got his wish. Perhaps it is another indication of that little piece of advice Whithouse is keen to follow; of leaving a scene as early as possible.

Another conscious decision in Whithouse's writing technique is to make his dialogue as natural as possible. Invariably this will mean stripping down lines to their bare essence. He often cites his experiences as an actor reading poor scripts as lying behind this emphasis[75], but amongst his sources of inspiration is Harold Pinter. The playwright's economy with words and observational realism about how people speak are also evidenced. This touching final scene between the Doctor and Amy is understated and almost too naturalistic as the denouement of a story that has only just brought

---

[75] E.g. Cook, 'The Nightmare Man', p20.

the viewers out of a mind-altering, sensually disorientating Kubrickian world.

The scene needs emotion, exposition and consequence, something to restore the viewer's empathy. Instead the characters' responses appear shallow and far too easy[76]. It's almost as if the episode ends with a Kubrick-like coldness, as if his philosophy has blended into a scene which should have been its undoing. Perhaps the problem lies in the fact that this is a false ending; the characters and the viewers know that there are more adventures to come. The Doctor is not ready to let go; the Minotaur within him lives on. Amy's faith in him is more problematic because the plot demands that it has been completely severed. Whilst the lure of the Volatile Circus is not met with the same response as that of the very tall men, is it plausible that a few brief words from the Doctor could completely cure Amy of her faith in the raggedy man, an obsession that led to her seeing numerous psychiatrists and counsellors as a child? At the very least there should be kicking and screaming, anger towards the man who apparently deceived an innocent little girl. The Doctor too remains strangely muted, considering his earlier outburst after Rita's death. Arguably the strength of Hurran and Whithouse's use of Stanley Kubrick's *The Shining* has compounded the issues with this closing scene, making it an unsatisfactory postscript to an otherwise intense psychological horror story.

---

[76] Slightly offset by Murray Gold's music score, which attempts to ratchet up the emotions.

I'VE MADE A TERRIBLE MISTAKE (AGAIN)

With such well-integrated external sources of inspiration establishing layers of meaning and context to *The God Complex*, it would be easy to overlook the episode's most natural reference point; the show's own past. Despite his modesty, Whithouse steeped himself in a thorough working knowledge of the **Doctor Who** mythology and back-catalogue. We have already seen the links with other stories featuring the Minotaur, which Whithouse either deliberately avoids, or uses as a throwaway continuity reference. But a number of familiar themes and storytelling conventions from other stories are brought to the table and used with varying degrees of licence. Most of them fall within the quintessential 'base under siege' format.

Bases under Siege

Toby Whithouse cites Russell T Davies's *Midnight* (2008) as one of his favourite **Doctor Who** episodes[77]. Elsewhere he argues that it is exactly the kind of story he aspires to write[78]. *Midnight* is one of the best post-2005 examples of the 'base under siege' trope; a regular story framework adopted in the series as early as the third serial, *The Edge Of Destruction* (1963). The name is slightly misleading in that it relates to a subset of this kind of story, used extensively in Patrick Troughton's era, where the base in question is literal and is usually staffed by a crew with an existing hierarchy of command. More broadly defined, this type of story is one in

---

[77] Alongside *Blink* (2007) (Cook, 'The Nightmare Man', p23).

[78] Martin, William, '10 Things We Learned from Toby Whithouse's Twitter Q & A'.

which 'the humans are in one room, the monsters in another, and the monsters are trying to get in[79].'

Sometimes disparagingly called little more than a money-saving device, the claustrophobic threat of a small group of people being trapped and hunted by an alien force in isolated surroundings presents great dramatic possibilities and compulsive viewing, especially if one by one those characters are picked off[80].Such plots, if handled badly, can reinforce good-versus-evil stereotypes and prejudices and turn the trope into a cliché. To an extent this is an unavoidable trap, given that the point of a good base under siege story is to exemplify the process by which evil 'feeds off the notion of otherness.'[81] Occasionally however, a story will subvert the cliché by shifting the real threat away from the monster of the week, or by presenting a more nuanced portrait of the enemy. *The God Complex* remains traditional in that respect, with the predator's pursuit of the characters relentless and unyielding. The Minotaur, despite its mythological hybrid roots, represents the anti-human, in that it kills by robbing a person of their individuality, cultural identification, and freedom of choice and expression.

A strength of these types of stories is that because of their limited settings and formulaic plots, the supporting characters tend to be among the most well defined[82]. It is therefore no surprise to find

---

[79] Sandifer, Phil, 'Q & A of the Damned'.
[80] E.g. *The Robots Of Death, Horror Of Fang Rock, The Unicorn And The Wasp* (2008).
[81] Decker, Kevin, *Who is Who? The Philosophy Of Doctor Who* (2013), p81.
[82] Decker, *Who is Who?*, p85.

Whithouse often settling on a format that allows him to place characterisation at the heart of his stories. Within this genre of **Doctor Who** stories, three in particular deserve special recognition since they share more specific parallels with *The God Complex*.

The Impossible Planet / The Satan Pit (2006)

A recurring feature of the base under siege story is that it often allows space for the writer to explore deeper questions of meaning. Faced with no way out, characters sometimes become introspective and philosophical with the spectre of death hanging over them[83]. Even if there is no opportunity for them to think, because of the constant need to run or build walls to keep the monsters at bay, those few that do survive, having been confronted by their mortality, invariably come out the other side with a more contemplative outlook on life[84].

In *The God Complex* the characters are frequently evaluating their lives, for better or for worse. Rita for instance, convinced that they are in Jahannam, consoles herself by reflecting on her past: 'Jahannam will play its tricks, and there'll be times when I want to run and scream, but I've tried to live a good life, and that knowledge keeps me sane, despite the monsters and the bonkers rooms.' Joe has reached the opposite conclusion: 'I have lived a blasphemous life, but he has forgiven me for my inconstancy.' Tragically, as they become increasingly possessed by the Minotaur, their judgements are proven to have been misplaced. They each begin to declare allegiance to the creature, with Howie stating that

---

[83] See for instance, *Midnight*.
[84] See especially *Last Christmas* (2014).

'nothing else matters.' Rory is uniquely unsusceptible to the conditioning process, but even he has cause to reflect, after being touched by Howie's success in overcoming his stammer, 'I'd forgotten not all victories are about saving the universe.' Once the puzzle has been solved and the TARDIS returned, Amy is eager to ask such fundamental questions of the Doctor: 'It didn't want just me, so you must believe in some god or someone, or they'd have shown you the door too. So what do Time Lords pray to?'

The last occasion on which such deep questions were posed to the Doctor, came, significantly, in *The Impossible Planet / The Satan Pit*, another base under siege story. Separated from Rose and with the TARDIS seemingly lost forever, the Doctor's conversations with Ida become increasingly existential.

DOCTOR

I didn't ask. Have you got any sort of faith?

IDA

Not really. I was brought up Neo-Classic Congregational, because of my mum. She was. My old mum. But no, I never believed.

DOCTOR

Neo-Classics, have they got a devil?

IDA

No, not as such. Just, er, the things that men do.

DOCTOR

Same thing in the end.

IDA

What about you?

DOCTOR

I believe... I believe I haven't seen everything, I don't know. It's funny, isn't it? The things you make up. The rules. If that thing had said it came from beyond the universe, I'd believe it, but before the universe? Impossible. Doesn't fit my rule. Still, that's why I keep travelling. To be proved wrong. Thank you, Ida.

Here the 10th Doctor reflects on how his rules limit his faith, and yet paradoxically spur him on to be challenged to think outside the box. His humanistic leanings are clear in the preceding line, where he views elements of religion and mythology, such as the devil, as symbols of the human condition. It is the search for knowledge that drives him on rather than any spiritual desire for enlightenment. The impossible will always have a scientific explanation, which might appear magical through ignorance, even to a Time Lord.

At the beginning of Steven Moffat's tenure, a conscious decision was made to move the show's tone away from its middling science-fantasy base, towards the magical end of the spectrum[85]. That isn't to say there was no longer a scientific explanation for the fantastical, but the 11th Doctor, unlike his predecessors, was not

---

[85] **Doctor Who** has always been more fantasy than science-fiction, but as the comprehensive study by Sean Nixon demonstrates, in the modern era Matt Smith's Doctor is the one most likely to face magical problems and offer magical solutions ('Is **Doctor Who** Science-Fiction or Fantasy?').

overly concerned with learning how or why things worked. *The God Complex* is an excellent case in point. The mystery of the Minotaur and its prison is not the result of lazy writing, because the Doctor shows no compulsion to explore the technology behind the ship or the physiological reasons or processes by which the Minotaur feeds off faith. He is far happier to embrace the unknown and work within its unfamiliar parameters. His pragmatic approach is such that all that matters is that he finds a way to escape the labyrinth and save as many people as possible in the process.

Unlike Ida, Amy fails to illicit a response from the Doctor. Perhaps this should be no surprise, given that he had earlier placed a 'Do Not Disturb' sign over the door to Room 11, keeping his fears, like his faith, well and truly hidden from sight. But it also functions to preserve the new level of mystery under Moffat's watch, with the seemingly jocular, carefree Doctor harbouring dark secrets.

Bad Wolf / The Parting of the Ways (2005)

Since 2005, the Doctor has demonstrated enormous care in his selection of companions[86], even to the point of rejecting the likes of Mickey (initially), Christina, Journey Blue and Me. To be fair, despite the apparent carelessness in allowing individuals to stow away on board the TARDIS, and in being taken in by Turlough, this has probably always been the case, rather than it being a

---

[86] The exception proving the rule being Adam Mitchell, taken in by the ninth Doctor after Rose Tyler's urging. His breach of trust after only one outing with the Doctor (*The Long Game*, 2005), reinforces the Doctor's 'I know best' mentality when it comes to selecting his companions. The working title for the Russell T Davies story was 'The Companion Who Couldn't' ('The Fourth Dimension').

consequence of some Time War trauma. But before the hiatus in the 1990s, it was never a concern of the writers. Whithouse of all the 21st-century writers has shown a particular interest in exploring the companion-Doctor dynamic and it can be no coincidence that he finds inspiration from the nearly companion, Lynda with a Y, in *Bad Wolf / The Parting Of The Ways*.

Whilst his default response to would-be fellow travellers is a resounding 'No', the Doctor has occasionally offered to take another person with him, in addition to those companions who already accepted the call. From the Doctor's perspective, the opportunity to join him is an irresistible temptation and he is genuinely surprised when he receives a knockback[87]. But in the case of Rita, the choice is taken away from both parties, uniquely paralleling Lynda's fate. Their respective deaths serve to add gravitas and trauma to the base under siege stories, teasing the viewer with the disturbing possibility that those even closer to the Doctor might not make it out alive. But they also challenge the assumed privileged status of Amy and Rose respectively[88].

In the climax to *The Parting Of The Ways*, Rose finds her position vindicated, despite the title of the episode hinting that she and the Doctor will be separated. After confirming her companion credentials by refusing her mother's counsel to let go of her hero,

---

[87] See for example, the ninth Doctor's reaction to Rose's initial but brief rejection (Rose), and the 12th Doctor's to Perkins (*Mummy on the Orient Express*).

[88] A theme that Whithouse also uses to good effect in *School Reunion*, where Rose meets Sarah Jane and discovers that she is just one in a long list of previous companions.

Rose returns to save the Doctor, triggering a reciprocal sacrifice and deeper bond (symbolised with the kiss of life). In stark contrast, Amy is effectively 'fired' by the Doctor. Viewers aware of Lynda's fate in the earlier story and of Rose's rollercoaster journey in which, following her apotheosis, a second assumed death is averted by the salvific kiss[89], will have been misdirected by Whithouse's script into thinking that Amy's position will be all the stronger by the end of the episode. The ending becomes all the more shocking as a result. But just as the ninth Doctor sacrifices his regeneration for Rose, the 11th Doctor – in an albeit far less heroic and decisive manner – is making a sacrifice of his own, precisely by letting go of Amy and Rory. As the Doctor says to the dying Minotaur, 'I severed the food supply, sacrificing their faith in me. I gave you the space to die.'

Horror of Fang Rock (1977)

Of all the base under siege stories, Terrance Dicks' *Horror of Fang Rock* is the one most obviously paralleled in *The God Complex*. Both stories hinge on the Doctor making a fundamental error.

Flaws in the Doctor's character, mistakes in his judgements and limits to his powers have been persistent features of **Doctor Who**, ever since viewers first shared Ian and Barbara's suspicions of the cantankerous and guarded first Doctor. For the first 25 years of the show, it was assumed that despite his alien nature, superior knowledge and advanced technology, he was nonetheless imperfect. Even when he was portrayed by Jon Pertwee as the suave, all-out action hero, there were still moments of vulnerability

---

[89] Her first 'death' being at the hands of the Anne Droid.

and weakness[90]. Only the fourth Doctor came close to being untouchable or at least perceiving himself as such; often combining his oratory skills with a quick-witted sleight of hand to topple his foes, he rarely seemed out of control. *Horror of Fang Rock*, however, turns on a monumental error of judgement by the Doctor and stands out for portraying the fourth Doctor as vulnerable as we have ever seen him. As if the producers felt this triumphalism needed to be put in check, the fallibility of the character comes to the fore immediately after Baker, with Peter Davison's less assured, more circumspect fifth Doctor. The shock of the *Fang Rock* twist would not have had so great an impact were it a Davison story. But despite the severity of the Doctor's mistake, it has no lasting implications on his character. It is assumed that the Doctor gets it wrong sometimes. His guilt is fleeting and we are soon travelling with him to the next adventure as if nothing bad had happened.

Since the late 80s the Doctor has been increasingly portrayed as a Godlike figure. With his fallibility no longer assumed, the wrongs of the Doctor are foregrounded by the writers as an issue, becoming grand statements about his identity instead of individual plot points. He has moved from being a flawed hero to being a fallen god. His mistakes are no longer one-offs; they are part of a bigger threat to the Doctor's being and carry graver significance for his followers. For example, the ninth Doctor blames himself for the genocide of his people; the 10th Doctor moves from utilitarian

---

[90] Before Matt Smith in *The God Complex*, the most explicit consideration of the fears of the Doctor came in the Pertwee years: see especially *The Mind Of Evil* (1971) and *Planet of the Spiders* (1974).

indifference[91] to Time Lord victorious[92] and is called out for both; the 11th Doctor faces up to the Dream Lord[93]; and the 12th Doctor spends a whole season questioning his morality, before concluding he is neither good nor bad[94]. A feature of modern **Doctor Who** is the irony that the godlike figure needs saving from himself.

The ninth Doctor deals with his guilt by filling up his time with as many 'fantastic' experiences as possible, looking to find reward in the actions of others. His unreserved joy when he declares, 'Just this once, everyone lives!' betrays the pain behind his seemingly carefree wanderings[95]. His salvation comes when at the end he is finally able to say that he too was fantastic[96]. The 10th Doctor's redemption is incomplete: he regenerates not wanting to go, but his guilt is partially assuaged by his farewell companion tour[97]. The 11th Doctor started out like a breath of fresh air, lacking the emotional baggage of Tennant and Eccleston, and confidently setting himself up as the defender of the Earth[98]. But this is a Doctor who, whilst embracing his assumed responsibilities, desperately tries to eschew his otherness, as if ashamed of being a Time Lord. He wants to be human, a cause for much observational humour in series five (2010) and six (especially with the Craig

---

[91] *The Fires of Pompeii* (2008).
[92] *The Waters of Mars* (2009).
[93] *Amy's Choice*.
[94] 2014, culminating in his revelatory speech in *Death in Heaven*.
[95] *The Doctor Dances* (2005).
[96] *The Parting of the Ways*.
[97] *The End of Time* part 2 (2010).
[98] *The Eleventh Hour* (2010).

Owens episodes)[99] as he makes various faux pas and fails to properly integrate. But ultimately, the 11th Doctor ends up becoming the most godlike of all his incarnations, sacrificing himself in order to save the universe[100]. It isn't until *The God Complex*, that the Doctor once again realises he needs redemption.

In series six, Steven Moffat boldly attempted to run two new arcs[101], putting on hold some of the outstanding questions of series five[102], keeping them in reserve to wrap up the 11th Doctor's story in series seven (2012-13). It also sets up the arc for series seven[103]. Viewed in the context of all these ongoing concerns, *The God Complex* is a frustrating episode. There is no direct reference to the Doctor's death and only one throwaway line concerning River Song. It will be retrospectively tied into the series five arc with *The Time Of The Doctor*'s (2013) revelation that the Doctor sees the crack in the wall in Room 11, but there is little foreshadowing of what is to come in series seven[104]. The fact that *The God Complex* was

---

[99] *The Lodger* (2010), *Closing Time*.

[100] *The Big Bang* (2010). Cf. The Fourth Doctor, *Logopolis* (1981), although whilst perhaps inevitable his fall from the dish is still accidental.

[101] The death of the Doctor and the identity of River Song.

[102] The cracks in time and the voice in the TARDIS. Whilst the Silence/Silents are introduced as an actual race in the opening two-parter of 2011 (*The Impossible Astronaut / Day of the Moon*), their precise nature and function is not properly spelt out until *The Time of the Doctor*.

[103] 'Doctor Who?'

[104] A noticeable difference between Russell T Davies and Steven Moffat's tenures is the use of prophecy and premonitions by the former.

originally written for the previous series might therefore indicate that it is a moveable feast[105], a standalone episode whose plot, aside from the departure scene, would have fitted into series five. But with the awareness of his own mortality hanging over him, the story placement is perfect insofar as it highlights the Doctor's fallibility; his propensity to jump to conclusions; his assumption that he can save everyone; his hubris, and his fears and insecurities.

The reversal in fortunes in *The God Complex* so resembles *Horror of Fang Rock* that the latter must surely have been an inspiration to Whithouse. In both stories, the Doctor makes a terrible mistake, thinking his actions are saving people when in fact he is condemning them to their deaths. But the implications run far deeper in *The God Complex*, to the extent that the Doctor decides that he can no longer continue as before.

The base under siege format is perfectly suited to both Whithouse's original spec and his early decision to use the location as a metaphor for the Doctor's wanderings, and the creature as a window through which the audience might reassess his character. The first line of script that Whithouse wrote, 'death would be a gift', formed the basis for the whole tale, revealing that this re-evaluation is the primary concern of the story[106]. The propensity for base under siege stories to include moments of deep existential reflection, so as to provide much-needed respite from the relentless pace and claustrophobic setting, provides Whithouse

---

[105] It was held back due to similarities with other stories, especially *The Time of Angels / Flesh and Stone* (2010) which also features a labyrinth.
[106] Pixley, 'The God Complex', p8.

with a ready-made genre in which to tease the viewers' expectations, by never quite revealing the Doctor's fears and faiths.

The shorthand approach to creating sympathy with characters by making them potential companion material is also stock base under siege fare, and neatly serves Whithouse's theme of the Doctor consciously relinquishing his hold over Amy. The tragedy of the death of almost-companions in the contained environment is exacerbated by them having been robbed of the chance to travel across all of time and space. And finally the plot device of making the hero's efforts to save counterproductive, in order to increase dramatic tension and delay or confound the resolution of the story, is again afforded the higher purpose of serving the heuristic dimensions of the story – in this case an exploration of the Doctor's vulnerability and fallibility.

Stories of Faith

Aside from the stylistic and thematic influences of the base under siege stories, a second group of stories to which *The God Complex* is linked thematically, are those which foreground faith.

The Curse of Fenric

Religion and faith have always placed an important role in science fiction and fantasy[107]. In a report to the BBC as an important part of the research undertaken before **Doctor Who** was conceived, two types of science fiction writings were identified: those that were straightforward, adventure stories set in space or/and the future,

---

[107] See McKee, Gabriel, *The Gospel According to Science Fiction* (2007), especially ppxi, xiii.

and those that explored fundamental questions of existence in which 'in a perhaps crude but often exciting way, the apparatus is used to comment on the big things – the relation of consciousness to cosmos, the nature of religious belief and such like'[108]. At the most basic level, religious beliefs and practices are used as critical elements in worldbuilding, but in countless short stories, novels, movies and television dramas, the dialectics between faith and science, spirituality and religion, and immanence and transcendence, have played central thematic roles[109]. Surprisingly, whilst replete with the former, **Doctor Who** has rarely strayed into more philosophical considerations of faith and belief, despite such concerns being standard sci-fi/fantasy territory.

The initial scepticism of the BBC over more speculative and philosophical science fiction, as well as their incredibly damning dismissal of CS Lewis ('we think [he] is clumsy and old-fashioned in his use of the SF apparatus [...] and his special religious preoccupations are boring and platitudinous'[110]), perhaps set the tone for the series. Somewhat patronisingly, the BBC decided that such a lofty matter was beyond the understanding and interest of their audience. A more cynical reading would suggest that an organisation, very much part of the status quo, was hardly likely to offend other traditional establishments or authorities. The show was expected to educate across a range of subjects in collusion with existing carriers of authority, such as church, school and state,

---

[108] Frick, Alice, and Donald Bull, 'Science Fiction: BBC Report'.

[109] For an extensive treatment of theology in science fiction, see McKee, Gabriel, *The Gospel According to Science Fiction*.

[110] Frick and Bull, 'Report,' 1962.

with morality and scruples being seen as more immediate than questions of faith, in that they could be more readily applied to everyday life, and could steer clear of controversy. It is a legacy that the institution and the show have found difficult to shake off. **Doctor Who** has more often than not played it safe[111].

The God Complex thus stands out alongside other exceptional cases, including *The Dæmons* (1971), *Kinda* (1982), *The Impossible Planet / The Satan Pit*, *Gridlock* and most noticeably *The Curse Of Fenric*, in directly tackling matters of faith and belief.

The Curse of Fenric is a clear influence on Whithouse, over and above the iconic scene in which the Doctor crushes Ace's faith. Whithouse writes that he has always been fascinated with deserted army camps[112]. *School Reunion* (2006) was originally to have been set near such a base, until Russell T Davies suggested the school setting. Whithouse finally got to incorporate such a location in his 2015 story, *Before the Flood*[113].

Curse, whilst riffing on tried and tested **Doctor Who** tropes, is another example of season 26's creativity, not only in the script, but in the way the story is filmed and edited. Very much a forerunner to **Doctor Who** in 2005, it explores the character of Ace in far more detail than had been the case with all of her predecessors, by fleshing out a backstory and examining how her travels in the TARDIS and friendship with the Doctor have impacted

---

[111] Notable exceptions in the political sphere include *The Sun Makers* (1977) and *The Happiness Patrol* (1988).
[112] Arnopp, 'Ghost Writer', p38.
[113] Whithouse notes how the setting for *Before the Flood* (2015) reminds him of *The Curse of Fenric* (Arnopp, 'Ghost Writer').

upon her. Whereas every one of her predecessors had departed suddenly, forcing more invested audience members into filling in the gaps with our imagination (e.g. by reading back Tegan's 'It's not fun any more' onto previous episodes), there was a real sense in season 26 that Ace's story was building up to something, and that finally we had a companion who was more than a replaceable servant to the plot and format of any given story. Had she left before the show was taken off air, it would have been a monumental episode, and not a quick and unexpected goodbye with a new motivation crudely added. Like Amy and Rory's departure in *The God Complex*, it would have been central to the plot and not tagged on as an afterword.

It is easy to see how this episode's treatment of Ace, coupled with the use of mythological creatures to highlight matters of the human heart and soul, would appeal to Whithouse's own sensibilities as a writer. And with that first line about the 'ancient beast' ringing around his head, the Doctor's dramatic encounter with Fenric would naturally have come to mind. Quite possibly, the inspiration for the idea of a creature who steals faith came from the Doctor doing exactly that to Ace. But the critical difference between the Doctor's attempts to break down the faiths of Ace and Amy, is that faith in *The Curse of Fenric* is positive, regardless of the validity of its object. It is an energy that keeps the demons away[114]. The Doctor is quick to rebuild Ace's faith, revealing that his psychological assault was tactical. In *The God Complex*, the Doctor

---

[114] By contrast, Whithouse's vampire story *The Vampires of Venice* (2010) shows the impotence of faith and its objects.

65

really means it. The message of the story is that blind faith in him, or any dogmatic belief system, is to be avoided at all costs[115].

It would be wrong to suggest that this change reflects an increasing secularism in **Doctor Who**. Even when the show was first conceived, Britain was experiencing a partial loss of confidence in the church as an institution. Scepticism towards its tenets of faith, born out of the two-pronged assault from scientific and technological advances and a relativising exposure to other belief systems, has been a constant backdrop to the series. But the idea that religion and belief can be **morally** wrong, whilst not new in itself, has certainly increased in emphasis in recent years, adding a new level of critique[116].

Post-2005, religion has been generally portrayed in a negative light because it is institutionally corrupt and manipulative[117]. In the very second episode of the revived series, *The End of the World* (2005), religion is banned on Satellite One, in the same breath as teleportation and weapons. Faith is equally scorned, whether

---

[115] For a fuller comparison between the breaking of Amy and Ace's faiths, see Jones, Tim, 'Breaking the Faiths in *The Curse of Fenric* and *The God Complex*', in Crome, Andrew, and James McGrath, eds, *Time and Relative Dimensions in Faith* (2013), pp45-59.

[116] No contemporary authorised guide will invite a bishop to supply a chapter on theology in **Doctor Who**, of the kind that appeared in the first edition of Hulke, Malcolm, and Terrance Dicks, *The Making of Doctor Who* (1972) (a chapter called 'Honest to the Doctor', a reference to liberal theologian Bishop JAT Robinson's influential work at the time, *Honest to God*).

[117] It is important to note however, that '**Doctor Who** has no default position on religion, whether positive or negative' Crome, Andrew, '**Doctor Who**: Time Travel Through Faith'.

because it is unverifiable by observation and at odds with science ('You're happy to believe in something that's invisible, but if it's staring you in the face, nope, can't see it. There's a scientific explanation for that. You're thick,'[118]) or because it is a forlorn and misguided quest for a false utopia, ('What if there's nothing? Just the motorway, with the cars going round and round and round and round, never stopping. Forever.'[119]). Although Steven Moffat re-establishes a role for the church, in militaristic form, its morals are ambiguous and the concept of the Silence as priests who make their subjects forget, suggests that the religiously mediated confession of sins might become a form of spiritual abuse, and allegiance to religion dependent on brainwashing techniques.

Despite the movement towards the fantastic since Steven Moffat took the helm, faith continues to be viewed critically. The absurdity of absolute, dogmatic faith is parodied in the Headless Monks: 'They believe the domain of faith is the heart, and the domain of doubt is the head. They follow their hearts, that's all.'[120] In contrast to other franchises such as **Star Wars** (1977-) and **Battlestar Galactica** (1978-80, 2003-09), the predominant stance of **Doctor Who** is one of healthy scepticism[121]. Faith in the supernatural and

---

[118] The ninth Doctor, *World War Three* (2005).
[119] The 10th Doctor, *Gridlock*.
[120] *A Good Man Goes to War*.
[121] It may indeed have once been a particularly defining British trait in comparison with the more positivistic views from the US. **Blake's 7** (1978-81) and **The Hitchhiker's Guide to the Galaxy** (1978-80) also present religion in largely negative terms. The rise of fundamentalism and the threat of terrorism on US soil has arguably

the religious mindset is stripped down to a story to live by. In **Doctor Who**, story is god. It does not matter if the stories have any factual basis[122]. They are judged either pragmatically, or on the basis of why they were created in the first place and how they might be used as a force for control or liberation. The Doctor is prepared to lie in order to instil hope, even if the object of faith is mistaken, as beautifully evidenced in a scene from *Flatline* (2014) when Clara is taking on the role of the Doctor while he remains trapped in the externally shrunken TARDIS:

                        DOCTOR

So what's next, Doctor Clara?

                        CLARA

        Lie to them.

                        DOCTOR

        What?

                        CLARA

        Lie to them. Give them hope. Tell them they're all going to
        be fine. Isn't that what you would do?

---

led to a more cynical approach, one more in line with classic British sci-fi (e.g. **Firefly** (2002)).

[122] Notice how the Doctor tells Howie, 'You're right. Keep telling yourself that. It's a CIA thing, nothing more.'

DOCTOR

In a manner of speaking. It's true that people with hope tend to run faster, whereas people who think they're doomed...

This tension between story and fact is clearly seen in *The Rings Of Akhaten* (2013). When Clara asks the Doctor if it is true that life originated on Akhaten, he replies, 'Well, it's what they believe. It's a nice story.' But by the end of the adventure, the Doctor is demythologising the people's god in a desperate attempt to save the Queen of Years from being sacrificed: 'It's not a god. It'll feed on your soul, but that doesn't make it a god.' He then proceeds to give a scientific explanation for the creation of life, but couches it in the form of a counter-narrative to their creation myth. It is a story to liberate and save: whether it is true, or not, or only partially so, it is one that highlights the self instead of the other, homing in on the uniqueness of the child. The Doctor then confronts the 'god' itself: 'Oh, you like to think you're a god. But you're not a god. You're just a parasite eaten out with jealousy and envy and longing for the lives of others.' As with *The God Complex*, the series seven story sees faith as a point of vulnerability, exploited by the powerful who set themselves up as gods, lords and masters.

Gridlock

Russell T Davies' *Gridlock* provides an interesting bridge between the positive role of faith in *The Curse of Fenric* and its devastating critique in *The God Complex*. There are clears parallels between Martha and Amy, with both of them declaring their absolute faith in the Doctor:

'...you haven't seen the things he can do. Honestly, just trust me, both of you. You've got your faith, you've got your songs and your hymns, and I've got the Doctor.'

[Martha, *Gridlock*]

'The Doctor's been part of my life for so long now, and he's never let me down. Even when I thought he had, when I was a kid and he left me, he came back. He saved me. And now he's going to save you.'

[Amy, *The God Complex*]

There are differences between the two companions' faiths in the Doctor – Martha's is without basis, irrational and foolhardy. She admits she knows little about him and that she has effectively sacrificed her family in order to travel with a stranger. Amy on the other hand, assumes that she knows the Doctor inside-out. But both are convinced that the Doctor is the only one who can save them.

Both Martha and Amy begin to worship with the others, with Martha joining in the chorus of 'The Old Rugged Cross' and Amy beginning to 'praise him.'

The Doctor however, rewards Martha's faith and breaks Amy's. The ending of the stories could not be more different. Martha finally gets to know something about her mysterious friend. He trusts her enough to begin to share about his own Gallifreyan path. It is a story of the Doctor's redemption, foreshadowed by Novice Hame's own redemption by the Face of Boe. The only one not to sing 'The Old Rugged Cross', the Doctor is instead struck by the guilt of having taken Martha with him: 'Hardly know her. I was too busy showing off. And I lied to her. Couldn't help it, just lied.' Martha shares a rare intimate moment with the Doctor, whilst Amy shares an awkward goodbye, with what is not said as significant as what is.

Seemingly far from having a god complex, despite having no faith allegiance of his own and 'going it alone,' the 10th Doctor acknowledges the Face of Boe as the true saviour in the story and praises Martha's ingenuity. After the stark portrayal of the futility of faith in the underground motorway network, the story is turned on its head by the revelation that the endless journey was for the travellers' protection, even if there was another way. Faith – though in a false, unreachable utopia – was literally keeping them alive, with a sense of purpose and community. Significantly, the reason for their tragic existence was the environmental aftereffects of a drug called 'bliss', suggesting that the pursuit of happiness in and of itself could lead to our destruction.

In *The God Complex*, faith is initially presented as positive, the one thing keeping the characters alive. In the end it has to be sacrificed, whereas at the end of *Gridlock*, it is redirected towards the present, symbolised in the singing of a new hymn, the distinctly non-eschatological 'Abide With Me'. *Gridlock* is thus far more quintessentially **Doctor Who** than *The God Complex*, in its positive affirmation of life. *The God Complex* runs with the darker tones of the earlier story, and takes Russell T Davies' undeveloped questioning of the Doctor's heroic status, here and elsewhere, to its logical extreme.

THE PSYCHOLOGY OF TERROR

Fear as the Overarching Theme

The various roles that fear plays in *The God Complex* extend far beyond the individual contents of the nightmare rooms. Even though the story turns from fear to faith, the latter is overshadowed by the former. Before being asked to spice up with a few set pieces what was initially a fairly cerebral and character-driven piece, Whithouse had already foregrounded the fear factor in Steven Moffat's original scenario of the hotel:

> 'Nowadays we have roller-coasters and **Doctor Who** to scare us, but maybe, hundreds of years ago that's why people had mazes – to give themselves that exciting little tingle of terror, to tap into that innate fear and thrill of being lost.'[123]

Fear operates on several levels in the story. The basic scenario the Doctor and his companions find themselves is in itself frightening. The primal, innate fears of death, being lost and being hunted by a fearsome predator provide the overriding tension of the drama. The personal, often quirky fears in the nightmare rooms add colour and individuality, blurring the edges between the viewer and the characters as we are invariably led to consider what would be in our own rooms. And finally, a culturally mediated fear from outside the prison and its occupants is directly referenced in conversation[124]. All this contributes to an assault on the viewers' emotions as we experience, in classic horror style, some of the

---

[123] 'An Interview with Toby Whithouse'.
[124] Fear of Islamic extremists.

physiological and emotional effects of being confronted by an object of fear. But this attack goes even further, as on an intertextual level we try to make sense of the story. There is little doubt that the role of fear in this story is not merely to engage the viewer in some kind of Aristotelian catharsis, but to leave us deeply unsettled and less secure by the end.

In the plot, fear is awakened in order to elicit faith. A function of the prison is to replace terror with belief. What matters most is the faith that is generated. Therefore, at its most basic level the story is about faith, not fear; an object lesson in how faith can do more harm than good. But for the viewer, the opposite movement takes place, as belief gives way to fear. Not only are we forced to doubt the value of another's faith, we are made to question the Doctor as the object of our own. We are even presented with the unnerving possibility of an unreliable narrator. Thus the show itself is open to question. Perhaps we should have left via the fire escape when Rory first encountered it, and switched over to **All Star Family Fortunes**. Perhaps that is our fear, that one day, like Tegan, we will find it stops being fun and we too will be looking for a way out.

We begin the story expecting the Doctor to find the way out of the maze. We trust that he will save everybody, with a few possible exceptions; there will be those who might bring about their own death, either by not listening to him or by an act of martyrdom. We share the Doctor's confidence that he will defeat, if not save, the Minotaur too. We assume clues have been placed along the way, whether from the conventions of the 'base under siege' genre, allusions to past episodes, or snippets of dialogue – only for the rug to be pulled from under our feet. For some viewers this makes *The God Complex* a deeply unsatisfactory episode. But the unanswered questions are deliberate and not an inherent weakness of the plot. It's not only the Doctor who has a god complex to shake. It is the show itself, the writer, the story and even we the viewers.

One of the reasons why fear inspires faith is because we are programmed to find order out of chaos. We have a need to make sense of the meaninglessness of life. We look for certainties, in situations when we would otherwise feel out of control. *The God Complex* ends with uncertainty, itself a root of fear. Is the Doctor giving up? Is this the end for Amy and Rory? What happened to River Song? How do they end up at Lake Silencio? What was that adventure all about? What was in the Doctor's room? What does he believe in? Why did Rory have no faith? The lack of proper resolution is compounded by the fact that despite the episode being thematically linked to the wider arc (which revolves around the most fundamental fear of all, the death of the Doctor), it never directly references it. That this was a deliberate creative decision can be seen in Amy's room not containing a flashback to the impossible astronaut. To do so would have made good sense as a way of representing the more obvious and immediate fear of the Doctor's death. Instead we see her waiting in vain for him as a seven-year-old. The most unsettling part of all is that because of the crushing exposure of the Doctor's fallibility we have recently witnessed, we are unsure whether we can carry these unresolved concerns over to future episodes. Has the fairytale with its promise of a happy ending been subverted by the depressing reality of the myth?[125] The viewer is faced with fears as to where this story might

---

[125] 'The pessimistic genre of myths creates suspense towards season finales and unsettle the viewer expectation of the happy,

74

be heading, fears to project onto the characters, the writers or even the show itself, yet the story we have just watched cautions us to resist falling back on faith as a way of overcoming them. Even to speculate about how the loose ends might be tied up, would make us like Howie, and look what just happened to him.

It therefore seems clear that *The God Complex* is playing with the emotions and responses generated by fear, not as an object lesson through characterisation but as a subjective experience for the viewer. On one occasion the didactic aims of Whithouse are made apparent. After the Doctor discovers that Rita is a Muslim, she jokes 'Don't be frightened'. Bertrand Russell famously critiqued religion for being based on fear, but the relationship goes two ways; fear provokes faith and faith provokes fear[126]. The central conceit of *The God Complex* is considerably undermined by the fact that faith can make a person afraid. It's all very well the ship projecting nightmares in order to awaken faith, but what about when faith itself has invented the nightmares? Crucially, Rita sees her overbearing father and not classic visions of Jahannam in her room. Is the concept of Jahannam, or hell, not invented as a means of control by manipulating people's innate fear of punishment and judgement? Whithouse was keen to present faith and fear as opposites, but in reality the relationship is far more complex. To get around this inconvenience, Whithouse characterises Rita as

---

fairytale endings that the Doctor's frequent bursts of optimism imply' (Malewski, Anne, 'Fairy Tales, Nursery Rhymes and Myths', in Barr, Jason, and Camille Mustachio, eds, *The Language Of Doctor Who* (2014), p206).

[126] For a good summary of Russell's views see Carlisle, Clare, 'Is Religion Based on Fear?'.

someone who does not fear Jahannam, and instead the use of fear as a tool to manipulate, scapegoat and stereotype is not embodied by any character in the drama, but drawn out in this line of dialogue.

In the wake of 11 September 2001, the relative peace after the end of the Cold War has been disturbed by a new fear, and politically based narratives that promote distrust and fear of the other have led to the demonisation of certain religions and peoples by large sections of the Western media. Nationalism is one type of faith that could have been represented by a character in the prison, with their nightmare room being filled with suicide bombers or Muslim women in burqas. But it would have led to the quite unsavoury and falsely propagated idea that the nightmare precedes the faith. The fears in the nightmare rooms, whilst personal and sometimes eccentric, are neither morally or intellectually questionable. Howie, for instance, might have been frightened of the opposite gender per se, but instead his room is filled with girls clearly teasing him. Fear itself, however, is a mechanism not to be trusted, insofar as it can be inculcated by people with vested interests. *The God Complex* steers away from this over-complication of its narrative and instead sets up scenarios of fears and faiths that have no obvious relationship or direct causal link to each other (e.g. Joe's fear of ventriloquists' dummies and his faith in luck. Even Howie, whose geekishness is linked to the teasing, has a faith in conspiracy theories rather than being, say, a Jediist). Faith is not used as a weapon against the nightmare, it is used as a form of escape, to distract the mind and provide focus, certainty and security in the face of a threat to existence.

In order to foreground fear in the viewers, *The God Complex* is crafted in the mould of a typical horror piece. We have already seen how *The Shining* forms an interpretive framework over the piece but by adopting that movie's setting and style, the horror genre as a whole also inevitably influences how we approach the experience.

Three Elements of Horror

Glenn Walters, in an insightful study of the horror movie genre, has identified three essential components to such stories; tension, relevance and unrealism[127]. The effectiveness of a horror flick depends on how well each element is adopted.

Tension

Different techniques are used in horror movies to create tension, such as the use of suspense, mystery, gore, terror and shock. They are the tools by which the viewer is drawn into the world of the story and the plight of the characters, in anticipation of a final resolution. Where the genre differs from action films is that the tension invariably involves 'the distortion of natural forms'[128], whether that be a supernatural force[129], or abnormal physicality[130]. Indeed many of the most memorable horror movies play on the uncertainty as to whether what is happening is supernatural or

---

[127] Walters, Glen, 'Understanding the Popular Appeal of Horror Cinema: An Integrated-Interactive Model', *Journal of Media Psychology*, Volume 9.2.
[128] Walters, 'Understanding the Popular Appeal of Horror Cinema'.
[129] E.g. *The Exorcist* (1973).
[130] E.g. *Jaws* (1975).

symbolic[131]. *The God Complex* is for obvious reasons low on gore and shock, but nonetheless fits the horror genre through the suspense of keeping the Minotaur in the background or only glimpsed fleetingly in reflections for as long as possible, and by the mystery of the ever-shifting corridors and 80s-themed hotel in space. Both the creature and the ship are 'distortions of natural forms.'

Relevance

Walters argues that in order to be watched, a horror movie, like any other, has to be relevant. It must relate to situations and characters immediately familiar to the audience. There are four levels of relevance: the universal, cultural, subgroup and the individual.

Universal fears in *The God Complex* include the unknown, loss, death and abandonment.

Cultural concerns are reflected in the changing themes of horror movies over the years. **Doctor Who** has often picked up on contemporary fears[132]. We have seen how *The God Complex* deliberately avoids such issues insofar as they might undo its fear vs faith dialectic, but nonetheless the character of Howie reflects the strong popularity of conspiracy theories[133]. Equally topical are

---

[131] E.g. *The Shining, Psycho* (1963).

[132] The most recent example being *The Zygon Invasion / The Zygon Inversion* (2015) which directly addresses worries over immigration, terrorism and religious extremism.

[133] The week before *The God Complex* was broadcast marked the 10th anniversary of the twin towers attack. *The Guardian* ran a feature on the numerous conspiracy theories about the atrocities

the hotel's surveillance system[134], and the (albeit brief) dialogue between Rita and the Doctor around Islamophobia.

Subgroup concerns more narrowly limit the appeal of a particular movie to a specific age group, very often adolescents. Such movies are often set in familiar surroundings for their target audience and play on important identity issues. All but one of the people encountered by the Doctor and Amy and Rory are contemporary British[135], but in keeping with the wide scope of the **Doctor Who** audience, they are taken from completely different walks of life. There is a tendency among some fans of **Doctor Who** to artificially set themselves apart from the general viewer. But the fact that many do feel a shared identity, to the extent of setting up a false dichotomy between the 'We' and the 'Not-We'[136], suggests that the character of Howie might well have been intended to represent such a sub-group. Although not unique to the 21st-century iteration of the show[137], ever since Clive represented the old-school fan[138] there has been a regular run of supporting characters who

---

committed that day (McGreal, Chris, 'September 11 Conspiracy Theories Continue to Abound').

[134] A few months before the transmission of *The God Complex*, the BBC ran an article titled 'Is CCTV Creeping too Far?'. Two years earlier the influential campaign group Big Brother Watch was established in the UK.

[135] Rita's Britishness is deliberately emphasised by the tea-making comment.

[136] The term is prevalent on various fan forums, e.g. Gallifrey Base.

[137] Whizzkid, *The Greatest Show in the Galaxy* (1988).

[138] See Arnold, Jon, *The Black Archive #1: Rose* (2016), p26.

quite explicitly embody certain aspects of fandom[139]. Whilst not a fan of the Doctor, Howie fits into the stereotype. Indeed, the original character notes confirm this was very much intentional: 'Young, shambolic, T-shirt and jeans and trainers. Pale. A mouth breather. Any similarity between him and fans of a certain science fiction show are purely coincidental.'[140]

Personal concerns are those which hook the viewer by encouraging them to identify with a particular character, sympathising with them at the expense of others who might, in their view, deserve their fate. The alien Gibbis is deliberately included as an unsympathetic character, and though originally written as a human[141], it is easy to see why he was the one selected to be alienised by Whithouse. Despite softening the character in the process, Gibbis remains dislikeable. The viewer might identify with one of the leads, or even with Howie or Rita, but is unlikely to sympathise with a character as submissive as Gibbis. The Tivolian's culture is one that would have welcomed the Minotaur's race. Gibbis therefore represents the opposite extreme to the unknown revolutionaries who have overthrown their Minotaur oppressors. It would have been truer to the conventions of horror if Whithouse had written Gibbis as a character sympathetic to the Minotaur's predicament who ended up sacrificed. Instead Whithouse uses

---

[139] Malcolm (Planet of the Dead, 2009), Osgood (introduced in *The Day of the Doctor*), Elton and LINDA (*Love & Monsters*, 2006), Lorna (*A Good Man Goes to War*).
[140] Pixley, 'The God Complex', p11.
[141] Pixley, 'The God Complex', p8.

Gibbis as another way of subverting the genre, by having him survive, unredeemed by the experience[142].

The script continues to play with the viewer's expectations, offering one last chance of a resolution. Gibbis speaks tenderly with Rory about his home world, seeing it through the portal. He then asks for a lift home. Perhaps the character could survive and still receive his just deserts, if the Doctor instead drops Gibbis off to another planet under subjugation by the Minotaurs. The viewer is deliberately robbed of any resolution to Gibbis' story, with the sudden jump cut to the Doctor dropping off Rory and Amy instead.

To feel personally engaged by the story and satisfied by its climax, the viewer needs to have redirected the emotions generated by the horror, towards the perpetrator[143]. However, since the Minotaur has been portrayed as a victim and as willing its own death, there is no fist-pumping moment of the kind we experience in a horror-movie resolution. By robbing us of a nasty or ironic fate for Gibbis, the least sympathetic character fails in that respect too. We are forced to either scapegoat the Doctor, or accept the lack of closure.

Unrealism

In order to be watchable, horror movies must maintain a balance between being readily relatable to real-life characters, situations

---

[142] In this respect Gibbis is not unique in the modern series: see also Rickson Slade (*Voyage of the Damned* (2007)) and Fenton (*Flatline*).

[143] This process is known as 'excitation transfer' (Zillman, Dolf, 'Excitation Transfer in Communication-Mediated Aggressive Behaviour').

and environments, and signalling to the viewer that they are works of fiction. There has to be an element of unreality or hyper-reality about the movies to make them palatable, even if that means using excessive gore and violence. *The God Complex*, both in the story elements and the way in which it is filmed, makes clear to the audience that its world is unrealistic. Though the creature is very real within its environment, the whole setting is a fabricated reality. Both the victims of the Minotaur and the occupants of the nightmare rooms conform to exaggerated comic-book stereotypes, reminding us that they are fictional characters[144]. In case the nightmares seem all too familiar to us, we are reminded that what we are watching is not real, with some uncanny directorial moves. The ventriloquists' dummies, for instance, break out of their limited function to scare Joe and become watchers over the dead, as if attending a vigil. The clown subverts himself by having a sad expression[145]. Both Howie and Rita are portrayed using common prejudices and assumptions. Howie, the fanboy, is a bespectacled virgin wedded to his PC. Rita the Muslim, with her results-driven father, could have walked straight off the set of **The Kumars at No. 42**. Despite praising the rare appearance of a Muslim in **Doctor Who**, one Islamic blogger is particularly scathing in her criticism of Rita's role in the episode:

> 'The only reason she's Muslim is to tell a cheap, albeit funny, joke and to have an example of someone with a deep faith for God. [...] a [Muslim] medical student who loves tea and

---

[144] Rita's father for instance, comes across rather like Christopher Lee's Dr Wilbur Wonka in *Charlie and the Chocolate Factory* (2005).
[145] The horror of a clown is its fixed smile.

whose greatest fear is disappointing her horribly overbearing father who can't accept her "B" in mathematics – are all convenient and unfortunate generalisations.'[146]

Gibbis' whole race is a parody of the weak-willed, unimaginative plodders whose faith in an outside agency is absolute. At first he is a comedic character, but just as the fears become increasingly less humorous (from the fear of socks to Room 11) a darker undertone slowly emerges. The Doctor initially accepts Gibbis' species and personality without critique, but as the tension increases and the threat closes in on them, he suddenly turns on Gibbis, with a harsh assessment of his race: 'Your civilisation is one of the oldest in the galaxy. Now I see why. Your cowardice isn't quaint, it's sly, aggressive. It's how that gene of gutlessness has survived while so many others have perished.'

These stereotypes remind the viewer that we are watching fantasy and that the deeply emotional message underlying the story is secondary to its focus on entertainment.

Three Sources of Irrelevance

Of the three elements of good horror, *The God Complex* works brilliantly when it comes to creating tension and unreality, but is far less effective in drawing the viewers into its world through relevance. There are three reasons why this might be the case.

The Inclusive Audience of the Show

Whithouse, whilst agreeing with Moffat that there is nothing wrong in scaring children, nonetheless censors his ideas appropriately for

---

[146] 'WoodTurtle', 'The Doctor Who Muslim Fail'.

a pre-watershed audience: 'There's a fine line between giving children that exhilarating scare, and utterly traumatising them.'[147] Not all young children are able to distinguish between fantasy and reality, therefore the unrealism in children's horror needs to be accentuated and the identification lessened[148]. But there is a more positive reason why a horror story aimed at children might veer more towards the fantastical than the horrific. Sam Leith observes that fear in children's literature is distinctly open and ambient – more unsettling than scary. Citing Maurice Sendak's *Where the Wild Things Are* as an example, he describes this effect as 'unheimlich', a German word meaning 'unhomely':

> 'These stories are a way of leaving the safety of home for a world created by someone else's imagination, where you are under their control. Suddenly, your bedroom is a forest. Suddenly, you are in a savage carnival. Of course it's scary.'[149]

The God Complex does exactly that.

The Fear and Faith Dialectic

The reactions to the nightmares are difficult to identify with, given that they are rather forced distraction tactics. In reality not everyone would turn to faith when faced with their greatest fear. The more natural response would be to freeze, to take flight by

---

[147] Cook, 'The Nightmare Man', p24.
[148] Arguably, children brought up as religious, find such distinctions more problematic than their secular peers (Waldman, Annie, 'Echo Chambers').
[149] Leith, Sam, 'Do You Know What Today's Kids Need?'.

hiding, or to lash out – whether against the threat itself, the environment, other people or oneself. Although each defence mechanism has been apparently tried by Rita and the others, it is not made clear that the appeal to faith we have already seen in the first scene with Lucy Hayward is a last resort.

A more positive response, often seen in situations of high threat, would be to draw support from each other[150]. The group encountered by the Doctor, Amy and Rory come across unnaturally because of a lack of comradeship between them. They are together, yet still acting and thinking as individuals. As soon as we are introduced to the tied-up Joe, with no proper explanation as to why the others have taken such a drastic step[151], it becomes clear that their reactions to being dumped into an alien and hostile environment are, perhaps not surprisingly, out of the ordinary.

The faith vs fear dialectic has little psychological plausibility, and ironically has more in common with evangelical discourse than it does with reasoned and sceptical challenges to religion[152]. At a stretch it could be argued that the alien ship has the power to influence how the arrivals respond to their fears, but if so it begs the question, why did it not project images of faith in their rooms? Perhaps part of the explanation for this unlikely scenario of using

---

[150] McGonigal, Kelly, 'How To Make Stress Your Friend'.
[151] Dialogue in which Joe asks to be tied up was cut (Pixley, 'The God Complex', p15).
[152] Evangelicals are frequently contrasting fear with faith (e.g. Witherington, Ben, 'Fear-Based Thinking Vs Faith-Based Thinking'), masking the role fear plays in faith.

nightmares to induce faith is the fact that they were a last-minute addition to the script.

Upsetting the Horror Genre

A third reason why *The God Complex* is weak on relevance, is that the story subverts the genre it borrows from. Just as the viewer expects the Doctor to be the hero, so too they expect that moment when they can exuberantly let out a cheer of emotional relief as the evil is overcome in the end. This process is well illustrated within the story, when the characters' heightened emotions, having been originally awakened by their fears, are quickly redirected into equally intense expressions of worship for the Minotaur. Physiologically similar effects take place in situations of extreme threat and pleasure[153], and in the case of Joe it is hard to pinpoint where one replaces the other. In any good horror movie, the viewer will go through a similar process, moving from intense fear to a corresponding degree of pleasure.

In *The God Complex*, that moment of triumph does not come. Residual heightened emotions that might have been born out of fear have nothing within the drama to replace them. Instead we are confronted by a creature who dies because it wants to, a hero who has made a fatal error of judgement and now doubts himself, and an understated scene where he says goodbye to the two people we thought might be significant in preventing his death later in the series. Worse still, Rory is filled with a schoolboy delight at his new car, and Amy is more struck by the fact that the Doctor is

---

[153] See Gander, Kashmira, 'Halloween and Horror Films: Why do we Enjoy Being Scared?'.

saving them than she is by the still unresolved problem of his apparent death in the near future. This intentionally dissatisfying ending adds a new level of intrigue, but only for those who can be bothered to carry on spinning plates of interpretation and speculation. For the rest, it leaves an awkward lack of resolution and a resignation to the incompleteness of the story.

If Whithouse had remained truer to the horror genre and hit the viewer with greater relevance, then arguably the ending would have been even more incongruous and unpalatable: 'The fear experienced by a viewer in response to watching a horror film is directly proportional to the viewer's level of sympathy for and identification with the protagonist.'[154] The episode relies on sketches and archetypes for its supporting characters and forces viewers into asking questions of the main characters instead of empathising with them. The need to leave huge question marks over the Doctor's, Amy's and Rory's characters, emotional states, relationships and future, has to limit the effectiveness of the horror. It would be against the rules to scare and not provide reassurance. The nightmares in *The God Complex* could only go so far.

Fear and the Minotaur

The Minotaur, perhaps more than any other mythical beast, has been interpreted by psychologists as a cipher for human fears. He is variously seen as an objectification of such primal fears as the unconscious, the unknown, nonexistence/death and instinct[155]. If

---

[154] Walters, 'Understanding the Popular Appeal of Horror Cinema'.
[155] Diamond, Stephen, 'Why Myths Still Matter'.

the creature is as fearsome as the legend makes out, and represents the innate, universal fears that Whithouse sought to illustrate, then why does it need to channel other fears in order to awaken faith? Why isn't the Minotaur itself behind every door in the prison? As we have seen in 'The Minotaur and His Maze', Whithouse draws upon the revisionist versions of the story, which look to find sympathy for the misunderstood and abused creature, and one way of overcoming fear is to disempower it by changing the narrative. The Doctor finally catches up with the beast in the Pasiphaë Spa. Commentators have been quick to spot the reference to the Minotaur's mother, but the type of room is significant too. One of the most instinctive responses to fear is to groom[156], so it can be no coincidence that this room is a spa. But whose fear is being symbolised? The Doctor at this stage is curious and unafraid, completely convinced he can save the others. The fact that this is the resting place of the Minotaur, before he begins his hunt, suggests that the fear is his. He is like a rat caught in a cruel experiment, unable to escape from his tormentor. Whereas once the creature proudly worshipped itself and its race, now it fears what it has become.

The prison was linked to the creature's psyche, bringing it a regular food supply in the form of worshippers, but now it has developed a fault. The reason and the nature of the fault are not explained, only one symptom of it, the leaking of the nightmares both temporarily and spatially from previous victims' encounters. If the creature has been driven insane, that perhaps that is what caused the ship to

---

[156] Gray, Jeffrey Alan, *The Psychology of Fear and Stress* (1971), p48.

malfunction. Perhaps the nightmares the ship projects in order to 'cook' the food source, are part of the fault. Instead of bringing faith direct to the creature, the ship mirrors the creature's own movement from belief to fear. Whether or not this conjecture is correct, there is no doubt that the idea that the ship is faulty can potentially cover a multitude of inconsistencies and unanswered questions, a helpful conceit for a single-episode adventure which required quite a radical rewrite.

Types of Fears

Fear has been defined and classified in various ways by psychologists, and every model must be treated with a degree of provisionality. Nonetheless it is helpful to identify and map the various processes that take place to make a person scared. Gray's fivefold codification provides a helpful way of classifying the various fears that feature in *The God Complex*, demonstrating the comprehensiveness of its treatment within the story[157].

Fears Derived From the Intensity of a Sensation

Such fears include loud noises, bright lights, the dark, excessive speed and other extraordinary attacks upon one or more of the five senses. These primal fears all trigger an intense feeling of being out of control, and are tamed either by repeated exposure or, in the case of infants, by the protection of a parent. None of the characters in *The God Complex* are directly confronted by this type of fear in their rooms, since maturation usually prevents them from becoming phobias. But such scares can still make us jump, before

---

[157] Gray, *The Psychology of Fear and Stress*.

we quickly adjust. They are disconcerting and shocking even when expected (such as a roller-coaster ride). In *The God Complex*, jump-cuts and the sound of the approaching Minotaur startle the viewer, and disorientating camera angles and panning shots make us dizzy.

Fears Derived From the Novelty of the Situation or Object

This is where the fear of the other derives from, such as strangers, people of other cultures, the opposite gender, or those who might challenge our assumptions about what is normal. Aside from the reference to Islamophobia, Howie's fears are very much centred around those who are different from him. But his stammer adds an interesting twist. It is a common misconception that those with a stammer are smitten by a nervous, fearful disposition. A phobia of stammering can be diagnosed, but the stammer itself is a genetic, neurological condition[158]. The girls who mock Howie themselves exhibit fear of his condition and suggests that part of Howie's fear was that it might one day return. 'You know, Howie had been in speech therapy. He'd just got over this massive stammer. What an achievement. I mean, can you imagine? I'd forgotten not all victories are about saving the universe.' The fact that his stammer does not fully resurface in *The God Complex* shows that it is not primarily triggered by fear and might be a helpful message to any viewers who might be battling with the same condition.

Within this category we might also include what Freud called the uncanny. Something that is familiar yet also unfamiliar can be even more disturbing because it represents the unknown breaking into the known: 'The uncanny explains a lot of horror tropes, where you

---

[158] Drayna, Dennis, 'First Genes Found for Stammering'.

look at something and it's not quite right — like a human face that's decomposing. It's recognisable, but just enough away from normal to scare you.'[159] The clown[160] and the ventriloquist's dummy[161] have become almost stereotypical forms of the uncanny[162]. The use of the clown in *The God Complex* also taps into more recent stranger-danger fears, when Amy pointedly says 'don't talk to the clown.'

Fears Derived From Evolutionary Factors

One explanation behind the apparent irrationality of many fears which are not triggered by a painful experience, is that they are rooted in the evolutionary development of our species. It explains why snakes and spiders elicit more fear than guns and cars, for instance. Certain mannerisms are triggered automatically when in a threatening situation and bear no discernible purpose. Originally they would have been essential strategies for survival, functioning to ward off a predator (such as the smile, yawn or frown). Almost all of the victims of the Minotaur confront the creature with a manic smile, suggesting that faith has not replaced fear, but sits alongside it. Rita appears to be fearless and unafraid, but in reality

---

[159] Goldhill, Olivia, 'Why Are We So Scared of Clowns?'.

[160] E.g. Pennywise (*It*, 1990), Clown doll (*Poltergeist*, 1982).

[161] E.g. Chucky (*Child's Play*, 1988), Billy (*Dead Silence*, 2007).

[162] Both clowns and creatures inspired by ventriloquist dummies have featured in previous **Doctor Who** stories. The former appear in *The Greatest Show in the* Galaxy and **The Sarah Jane Adventures**: *The Day of the Clown* (2008) and *The Nightmare Man* (2010); note too that the Doctor identifies with George's fear of clowns in *Night Terrors*. The latter are incorporated as Mr Sin in *The Talons of Weng-Chiang* (1977) and the Smilers in *The Beast Below*.

it is not fear that has been defeated, but its effects. She is not frightened by her fear. It is the difference between terror and awe. Gods are almost universally portrayed as beings to be loved and feared in equal measure. Such fears tend to lurk below the surface and are triggered in association with other, more immediate threats. Lucy Haywood's burglar, for example, is dressed in a gorilla suit. The whole premise of *The God Complex*, being hunted by an animalistic predator, harks back to this primal fear.

Fears Derived From Social Interactions

In Gray's model, such fears are again innate and are linked to issues of dominance vs submissiveness. Through sign-stimuli, individual members of a species claim their territory and/or partnerships for the purpose of procreation. Fear is a natural response to any attempt to challenge territory by a member of the same species. Both the defender and attacker experience fear in order to maintain and reinforce existing boundaries. The inherent danger, when applying such a model to human relationships, is that it could be used to reinforce or naturalise gender and class stereotypes. Inherited fears and socially-conditioned fears are not so neatly divisible, since they feed off each other. A conditioned response passed down through the generations can appear innate. Instead of distinguishing between the two on the basis of a misleading innate vs acquired division, it is better to think in terms of implicit socialisation vs explicit social conditioning.

Specific fears rooted in implicit socialisation are those of isolation, loss, rejection and abandonment. Sigmund Freud argued that this is the basis for what he termed the herd instinct, or going along with the crowd. One disturbing theory regarding the appeal of horror movies is that is that when watched by a mixed gender group, men enjoy the movie more if the women are visibly scared, whereas women enjoy the movie more if the men show a lack of fear[163]. The 'snuggle' theory sounds inherently sexist and yet is demonstrably true because of socialisation. But watching a horror movie is an exercise in role-playing, and reassuringly it has little basis in real-world responses to fear triggers: a social history of fear in 20th-century Britain and the USA has shown that men are the more timid[164].

In *The God Complex*, the male companion appears at first to be fearless, and a conversation between Rory and the Doctor suggests that both assume this to be the case. But it should be recognised that Whithouse' starting point was Rory's lack of faith. His apparent fearlessness serves merely to misdirect the viewer into believing the Doctor's mistaken assumption as to what the creature feeds on. Rory's lack of a room was a symptom of a lack of faith, not fear. Indeed, the fire escape perhaps indicates his greatest fear: the fear of losing Amy to the Doctor and of leaving without them. Tellingly the Doctor picks up on Rory speaking in the past tense about his travels with the Doctor. For Rory, the running has already stopped[165]. Rory is a problematic character in series six, because unlike Mickey, he has become part of the fairytale. Whithouse sees

---

[163] The 'snuggle' theory of Zillman, Weaver and Mudorf, 1986, features in a comprehensive review of the field in Filmmaker IQ, 'The Psychology of Scary Movies'.
[164] Bourke, Joanna, *Fear: A Cultural History* (2005).
[165] Note how he only sees the fire escape when stopping to tie up his shoe.

Rory as the audience identification figure[166], but in reality he is as difficult to relate to as Amy.

Doctor Who since 2005 has shown a more enlightened view of gender differences, resisting the stereotyping of female companions and reflecting the reality that men are more likely to exhibit fear than women, such as Mickey, Rory (in series five) and Danny Pink. In *The God Complex*, the twist when the Doctor realises the creature feeds upon faith and not fear could have been used to challenge how the viewer sees Rory – for instance, by making Rory the character most fearful of the Minotaur when they finally encountered it. But detrimentally, there is nothing in the script to help us read back the Doctor's correction into the earlier scene.

Rory's fear keeps him travelling with the Doctor and Amy. Against his better judgement, he follows the herd mentality because he is driven to stand by his wife who shows no signs of wanting to stop running. At the most he challenges with a feigned humour, for fear that he will be shown the door. He is submissive in the relationship, hence the significance of the Doctor addressing them as the Ponds.

Whithouse has been criticised for the line in which the Doctor refers to Amy as 'Mrs Williams'. Phil Sandifer goes so far as to suggest it is 'the single most misogynistic moment of the Moffat era, and possibly of the new series altogether.'[167] He argues that by making this a part of the Doctor breaking Amy's faith in him, the implication is that her identity as Pond was part of her silly, fairy tale fantasies. But such criticisms fail to consider the Doctor and

---

[166] Cook, 'The Nightmare Man', p22.
[167] Sandifer, 'A Great, Great Partnership'.

Rory's role in the story. The Doctor is effectively signalling to Rory that he is not, after all, the also-ran. He was never really that for Amy; it was all part of the Doctor's hubris and god complex. Rory believed the Doctor more than he believed Amy. Addressing Amy as 'Mrs Williams' is about the Doctor giving up his ownership and control over her. It has nothing to do with Amy becoming submissive in her relationship. With the uncorrected assumption of Rory's fearlessness and stereotypical penchant for material things, it is unsurprising that the 'Mrs Williams' line also backfired.

Fears Derived from Classical Conditioning

Classical conditioning is the means through which an innocuous stimulus can generate fear through association. It is the root cause of most phobias. For example, a slipper, ruler or belt used in corporal punishment can become an object of fear, even when there is no discernible associated threat. Negative social conditioning artificially triggers exactly the same reaction, investing objects, people or situations with meaning by invoking a fear of consequences. The contents of the nightmare rooms in *The God Complex* are specific and mostly related to past experiences (classic conditioning). The trigger and the consequences feature together, to ensure that the episode does not move into the absurd or black humour. The portraits on the wall, however, suggest that the objects of other people's nightmares are sometimes detached from any negative consequence, encouraging the viewer to fill in the blanks with fears that are potentially much darker than could be screened pre-watershed (it doesn't take a huge stretch of the imagination to think up disturbing scenarios why somebody would be frightened of a camera). Anything can become monstrous. Even the Doctor.

THE FOLLY AND THE COURAGE OF FAITH

If fear is a difficult state to define, then faith is even more of a philosophical minefield. Before we can understand what implications *The God Complex* has for faith, it is important to unpack the meaning behind the word.

Faith is sometimes mistakenly reduced to the adherence to a set of doctrines - e.g. a belief **that** Jesus is the Son of God. But at the opposite extreme it can be interpreted in such a way as to make it indistinguishable from spirituality – e.g. a belief **in** Jesus as the Son of God. The one approach is objective and puts all the meaning on the contents of the beliefs, the other is subjective and places all the stress on how such beliefs impact on the individual. But faith defies either narrow definition. Worshippers are able to suspend their disbelief and avoid cognitive dissonance, keeping the faith when either logic or experience testify against it. Beliefs and lifestyle are intrinsically linked, even if to an outsider they might appear contradictory.

Faith is more fruitfully understood as a process rather than a system. It is the way in which we make sense of an otherwise chaotic, valueless existence and in that respect it is one of the most fundamental building blocks of socialisation. As a process, faith itself goes through different stages linked to developmental changes. The sociologist James Fowler identified six such stages of faith[168]. The first two are usually only found in young children,

---

[168] Fowler, James, *Stages of Faith: The Psychology of Human Development and the Quest for Meaning.*

being literalistic and non-reflective[169], so only the next four need concern us here.

Conservative faith[170] is typically displayed in adolescence and is characterised by an absolute trust in one's primary tradition. In the face of competing spheres of influence the person at this stage of faith development defends any potential challenge to their worldviews by an assertive reinforcement of inherited values.

Challenging faith[171] is a period of uncertainly facilitated by a loss of confidence and trust in the traditions handed down. The realisation 'it ain't necessarily so' fosters a period of angst and either a rejection of values and a loss of faith or an adoption of new values and a conversion to other causes or beliefs. It is a deconstructive time and leads to a deep suspicion of authority and structure.

Collaborative faith[172] is marked by a new positivity and an ability to hold in tension the previous two stages. Rather than seeing things as 'either/or' they can be 'both... and...' It is a relativistic mindset that allows for truth and meaning to be found both within and beyond handed-down traditions. The rejected symbols of the past are given a new lease of life, seen as metaphors rather than magic. A tradition can be both questioned and welcomed and whilst such

---

[169] See Fowler, *Stages of Faith*, pp122-150.

[170] I have avoided using Fowler's more technical terminology. Here conservative faith is the equivalent of Fowler's 'Synthetic-Conventional Faith' (*Stages of Faith*, pp151-173).

[171] 'Individuative-Reflective Faith' in Fowler's model (*Stages of Faith*, pp174-183).

[172] 'Conjunctive Faith' in Fowler's model (*Stages of Faith*, pp184-198).

a person stands within a certain tradition they are able to see and think outside the box.

Creative faith[173] carries the same philosophy as the collaborative stage but adds to it a sense of urgency and a compulsion to engage rather than to simply observe. Only a select few reach such lofty heights. Rather than merely respecting other traditions, such people have the capacity to learn from them and to incorporate new insights into their worldviews. They also dare to offer a third way by seeing beyond the black-and-white. Such faith brings about liberation, whether social, political or religious. Its holders have moved from a position of seeing to standing outside the box.

In every form of organised belief, both religious and secular, adherents will be scattered across these different faith stages (moving freely between them in both directions), even if it is in the vested interests of the institution to keep its members at the juvenile, unquestioning conservative end. When understood in this way, faith is neither the opposite of doubt (it doesn't necessarily involve accepting a set of propositions) nor mistrust (it doesn't require a relationship of total commitment to the object or transmitters of faith). Faith is an affirmation of life and creativity as a protest against the inevitability of death and decay. It is inherently optimistic in all its stages, whether naïve or critical. We have already seen that, contrary to what might appear to be the case *in The God Complex*, the opposite of faith is also not fear. Instead, the antitheses of faith include disorder, disharmony and

---

[173] 'Universalising Faith' in Fowler's model (*Stages of Faith*, pp199-210).

despair. A faithless state can be likened to a jumble of jigsaw puzzle pieces without any pattern to work towards. A person of faith has a framework or vision, to bring those mixed-up pieces into an ordered whole. The finished article need not be religious, and it need not make sense to the outsider. What matters is the dual processes of becoming and belonging.

Faith has past, present and future orientations, which could be described respectively as a stance, a mind-set and a quest. Take the character of Gibbis for instance. His stance, learned from his inherited tradition, is that the greatest good is to be subjugated and controlled. His mind-set is submissive, nervous, overly in awe of the other. In science fiction and fantasy, the most powerful of the three orientations is future-facing. This in turn can be divided into different types of quests – a quest for transcendence, meaning, truth, utopia or identity, all driven by a faith that the vision is attainable. Gibbis' quest is for the twisted utopia of subjugation by a new ruler.

In *The God Complex* it is not faith per se that is critiqued. It is both belief as a future orientation, and a particular stage of faith that feeds the Minotaur. Each person brought to the prison has a faith that is unquestioning and conservative and one that is striving for a future reward, whether it be divine favour on the day of judgement (Rita), credit for the successful unmasking of a conspiracy (Howie), striking it lucky (Joe), a new overlord (Gibbis), or ever more fantastical adventures with a hero (Amy). When faced with their deepest fears, faith provides those on board with a reassuring certainty, a powerful distraction, and a framework for interpreting the unfamiliar.

Since the Minotaur wants to be worshipped as the one true God, challenging, collaborative or creative forms of faith would not be so easily digestible. The Doctor, for instance, despite having a room in the complex, is not taken in by it. There is never a moment when the viewer is led to believe that the Doctor might start praising the creature. His faith is characterised by openness and a healthy provisionality, yet that in itself is his undoing, since it forms part of his god complex by giving him a sense of unlimited freedom.

By following this train of thought, Rory too is not completely devoid of faith. He is at the challenging stage of faith, indirectly questioning Amy's trust in the Doctor. By embracing the questions, he has almost reached the point of rejecting the TARDIS. The previous story marks the turning point, when he confesses '...I don't want to travel with you.'[174] Travelling with the Doctor brings with it a complicity that Rory cannot handle. Rory does not want to become like the Doctor, but he has no choice. He has to lie to Amy when she wakes up and asks about her older self[175].

Now that we have made distinctions between the various types of faith, it is possible to read the Doctor's breaking of Amy as an attempt to move her from the conservative to the challenging stage. Whithouse's next episode, *A Town Called Mercy* (2012) reflects this movement well, when Amy calls the Doctor to account.

---

[174] *The Girl Who Waited.*

[175] The previous story ends on an emotional cliffhanger, with Rory left to face Amy, who at this point does not know the fate of her older self. The fact that she is carrying on as normal at the start of *The God Complex* implies he probably lied to protect her faith in the Doctor.

It is not the first time Amy has questioned the Doctor of course, but after the events of *The Girl Who Waited*, her faith in him had become almost absolute, in contrast to the older Amy of the alternative timeline, who sarcastically calls him 'God' and confesses to hating him. Indeed, Old Amy's description of him as a 'blue-box man flying through time and space on whimsy' could have been his own in *The God Complex*, when breaking the younger Amy's faith.

Subconsciously, Amy is afraid that her faith in the Doctor has been misplaced – that one day he won't come back for her, ever – but that nagging fear is deliberately suppressed by faith. Fear therefore, though not the opposite of faith per se, is the shadow side of conservative faith. The tendency to reaffirm truths as objective certainties with evangelistic zeal, to preach this or that gospel, is a reaction to the inherent insecurity behind a faith that purports its object to be infallible.

The tragedy of the Minotaur's unnatural situation is that every time he acquires a new worshipper he kills them in the process. It is a similar irony to the one explored by Whithouse in the character of the vampire Mitchell in **Being Human**. So in one respect this bizarre situation serves to create empathy for the monster. But it is also a statement about the folly of conservative faith, for however sympathetically Whithouse intended to treat Rita, her belief is ultimately her undoing. She is not stereotyped negatively on account of her religion (she is neither a fundamentalist nor an oppressed woman); indeed the fact that she is a Muslim and not a Christian or a Jew is immaterial. But nonetheless, there is no doubt that her faith is absolute and therefore brings with it the inevitability of her death. In extreme cases, faith in the conservative stage can kill, needlessly so[176]. As a form of martyrdom in which nobody is saved it lacks any redeeming features. The deaths of Rita, Joe and Howie are a waste.

Howie's faith in conspiracy theories is also at the conservative stage and is therefore sharply rebuffed by Rory. Howie uses it to conclude that they have been transported to Norway:

> 'You see, the US government has entire cities hidden in the Norwegian mountains. You see, Earth is on a collision course with this other planet, and this is where they're going to send all the rich people when it kicks off.'

Unlike the existence of God, some conspiracies are proven facts. Faith in a conspiracy is not mistaken per se, but when it becomes a universalising way of understanding and relating to the world, such a belief ignores, forces, twists or invents evidence to support it. Michael Shermer suggests 10 characteristics that indicate a conspiracy theory is false. All of them apply to Howie's paranoid theories:

- a lack of evidence
- elevating the agents of the conspiracy to superhuman powers
- complexity and multiple elements
- too many people involved for it to remain secret
- too grand

---

[176] See for example the practice of snake handling, or the accidental deaths of several Ugandan Christians whilst being baptised in the Mugoya dam.

- smaller events ratcheted up to larger events
- sinister interpretations of innocuous events
- mingling fact with speculation
- indiscriminate hostility to government agencies
- the refusal to consider alternative explanations[177].

Joe places his faith in both superstitious/ritualistic behaviour and luck. Superstitions are clear examples of the human tendency to find patterns in unconnected objects and events. Making associations is essential to the survival of our species, a fact that the eighth Doctor found quaint: 'I love humans, always seeing patterns in things that aren't there.'[178] This aspect of faith is part of our evolutionary make-up:

> 'Whenever the cost of believing that a false pattern is real is less than the cost of not believing a real pattern, natural selection will favour the patternicity [...] people believe weird things, because of our evolved need to believe non-weird things.'[179]

Finding patterns is essential in both religion and science, and always highly contestable. Exceptions to the rules, other factors that influence the data, and the need to make generalisations from a set number of examples, should make any conclusions provisional, no matter how probable. Superstitious behaviour can be nothing more than a 'just in case' reaction, such as when

---

[177] Shermer, Michael, *The Believing Brain* (2011), p246-7.
[178] *Doctor Who* (1996).
[179] Shermer, *The Believing Brain*, p72-73.

avoiding walking under a ladder, but in its more extreme form, it is treated as essential.

Even when evidence linking cause and effect is lacking, a priori beliefs when formed within the conservative stage of faith insist that the pattern works. Sometimes it does by way of a placebo effect. Joe may well have been a more successful gambler when he wore his good luck charms, because he could think more clearly and weigh up risks and probabilities better[180]. Research has shown that people who believe in luck as a stable quality rather than an unpredictable, fleeting experience, tend to be more driven towards success[181]. The researchers hypothesise that the reason why such beliefs have positive effects is that they give the adherents a sense of control. How far a person thinks they are in control of a situation determines how confident they are, even if that control is an illusion (e.g. by throwing your own dice). There is evidence to suggest that compulsive gambling and irrational beliefs are often linked, and are symptomatic of flawed reasoning processes that are heightened in times of emotional stress[182]. When faced with his greatest fear and placed in a situation in which he feels out of control, unable to read the poker faces of the dummies that surround him, Joe turns to his superstitions, because they give him an albeit false sense of control and invulnerability. Luck 'may help

---

[180] 'Research has suggested that people who think of themselves as lucky actually are lucky, because they are more willing to take advantage of opportunities' (psychologist Mike Aitken, quoted by Lane, Megan, 'Why Do We Believe in Luck?').
[181] Dowden, Craig, 'Why You Should Believe in Luck'.
[182] Melina, Remy, 'Impulsive Gamblers are More Suspicious, Study Suggests'.

us coping with chance events, such as being involved in an accident, a mugging or natural disaster, as it can help people feel more optimistic when circumstances are beyond their control'[183].

The transformation of a person's faith into the worship of the Minotaur makes religious belief the big baddie of the episode, setting it apart from other forms of faith for special criticism. Even though, refreshingly, Whithouse considers faith in its more generic sense, it is notable that the Minotaur wants to be worshipped as a god and not believed in for any other reasons. There is no obvious reward on offer, and the different quests have all become a quest for transcendence, in which the self is completely lost in the other. The idea that encountering God will kill is found right across the religious traditions, both literally and symbolically[184]. The worship of the Minotaur is characterised as irrational and non-cognisant in the repeated cry of 'praise him.' But who is demanding that the Minotaur be worshipped?

Gods are usually worshipped as creators, whether of the whole of existence or one part of it, but a different creator lurks behind *The God Complex*. The whole situation has been entirely engineered by those who have imprisoned the creature. It is a clear statement about the role religion can play in limiting the freedom of others, by defining both faith and its object. In the same way that the Minotaur has become a tool for the civilisation who have

---

[183] Lane, 'Why Do We Believe in Luck?'

[184] In Christianity, for instance: 'You cannot see my face, for no one may see me and live' (*Exodus* 33.20), and metaphorically, 'whoever wants to save their life will lose it, but whoever loses their life for me will find it' (*Matthew* 16.25).

imprisoned it, so too the idea of God can serve to prop up an oppressive regime. The hidden horror of the prison is that it is being used to destroy the diversity of faith, by converting people to the one true/false God.

Although Gibbis, Howie and Joe do not present with religious beliefs, they each embody a pattern of faith that has been a particularly useful tool for religious institutions. It is these aspects of their beliefs that are converted into food for the Minotaur. They are irrational, conservative and future-orientated. Gibbis' slave mentality is a secular parallel to the kind of Christianity described by Nietzsche. The philosopher argued that Christianity was a religion of pity for the weak. As summarised by Vincent Brummer, Nietzsche believed that Christianity:

> '...makes a virtue out of weakness, humility, poverty, and abasement and prevents people from developing and becoming strong and noble. By idolising inferiority it keeps people inferior and dependent and makes them assume a slave-mentality.'[185]

Despite the protests of liberation theologians, the church continues to promote poverty as a virtue across all its denominations. Howie's conspiracy theories suggest that the world is not as it seems and that we are all being lied to. Instead of being comfortable in the present moment we should be preparing ourselves for the coming apocalypse. Christianity too makes bold, universal claims about the powers and principalities that rule this world, and prophesises about the end of days. Joe's superstitions

---

[185] Brummer, Vincent, *The Model Of Love* (1993), p141.

and use of charms are the secular equivalents of crosses, bibles and fish symbols.

The fact that Rita, the only person to belong to a religion, is the least parodied character and the hardest one to define, reflects the continuing unease towards explicitly critiquing religion on primetime UK television. But it is not difficult to find, for instance, a Christian equivalent to Gibbis, Howie or Joe.

Views of Religion

All of the individuals who die in the prison do so because they are converted to a new faith, but what does the manner of their transformation tell us about how the writer interprets religion? The implications are that religion can be a system of control, a symptom of mental illness, and a survival mechanism.

A System of Control

> 'The God of the Old Testament is arguably the most unpleasant character in all fiction: jealous and proud of it; a petty, unjust, unforgiving control-freak; a vindictive, bloodthirsty ethnic cleanser; a misogynistic, homophobic, racist, infanticidal, genocidal, filicidal, pestilential, megalomaniacal, sadomasochistic, capriciously malevolent bully.'
>
> [Richard Dawkins, *The God Delusion*]

The Minotaur matches none of these provocative descriptions of Yahweh. Instead he is characterised as being a prisoner without agency or control, a creature reduced to mere instinct who cannot but kill because that is the way he now is. And yet he takes absolute control over his victims, robbing them of their individuality, their fears and their faiths. From the victims' perspective the process is described as if it is a willing act of worship. The message is clear: religion takes control and manipulates people into going against their better judgement.

The Minotaur is not the true heart of the religion of the prison ship. The environment's God is itself: just as the church might invent a God in its own image, so too, the Minotaur's divinity is constructed by the vessel. The mind behind the prison is omnipresent, omniscient and omnipotent. In cases of domestic abuse, controlling behaviour typically manifests itself by the abuser keeping tabs on his victims, robbing them of their privacy. There is something deeply sinister underneath both the 'I'll be watching you' sentiments of *Psalm* 139 and Sting's 'Every Breath You Take'[186]. The same fear lies at the core of Orwell's *1984*. Similarly, in *The God Complex*, we are led to believe that every event and every person is being monitored by the CCTV system. The ship also appears to be omniscient, in that it knows its victims' deep and private secrets, and is able to force them to relive events that sometimes go way back into their past. Finally it is all-powerful. Any attempt by the victims to stay in control of their situation is met with supernatural resistance, such as the reconfiguration of the room layout, the turning back on of the muzak, and the splitting of the ties that bind Joe to his chair.

Worshipping the creature in the maze is expressed by every victim as the handover of control to a higher power:

---

[186] Being watched and/or stalked is a common horror movie cliché (e.g. *Scream* (1996), *Hush* (2016)).

'The gaps between my worships are getting shorter, like contractions.'

[Lucy]

'Nothing else matters any more. Only him.'

[Joe]

'…now I am blinded by his majesty. Humbled by his glory!'

[Howie]

'I can feel the rapture approaching, like a wave.'

[Rita]

Even though Rita is a Muslim, she uses a word derived from a branch of Christian theology to describe the arrival of the Minotaur[187]. Howie draws upon Christian traditions when he paraphrases the hymn 'Amazing Grace' by saying 'I was lost in shadows, but he found me.' Joe describes his conversion in Christian terms as 'I have seen the light', and Lucy's analogy to contraction has biblical precedent in the Johannine concept of being born again, and more specifically in *Matthew* 24.8 which likens the signs that the world is coming to an end to birth pangs. The repeated refrain of all those who succumb to the lure of the Minotaur's lair is a generic 'praise him'; a common phrase uttered spontaneously during prayers and sermons in charismatic and Pentecostal churches, and a repeated line in popular hymns such as

---

[187] The Rapture: at its crudest, the belief that on the Day of Judgement believers will be physically transported to heaven by Jesus, with the unredeemed left behind.

'Praise my Soul the King of Heaven'. Without making his criticisms explicit, Whithouse is clearly suggesting that Christianity, though ingrained in British culture, can nonetheless be a force for harm, especially in its conservative-evangelical form.

A Symptom of Mental Illness

Religion can have beneficial or harmful effects on mental health. Positively it can create a reassuring meaning, purpose and sense of belonging in life, dependent on the types of beliefs and social structures it promotes. It might even create positive placebo effects. But religion can also do harm, encouraging paranoia, escapism, recklessness and hatred of outsiders. It can lead to the avoidance of medical treatment through the misdiagnosis or denial of a condition and its cure or management. But sometimes religious belief is a symptom of a mental illness. A pre-existing paranoia might latch onto the language and practices of a religion, and voices in the head might become messages from above.

The character of Rita has been hailed as a positive role model for Muslim women in **Doctor Who**. On a surface level her faith is courageous and positive. At first she seems to be open to other possibilities, suggesting that she has passed the naïve and defensive conservative stage of faith. She is confident, assured and, in the Doctor's words, 'clever'; all the things he looks for in a new companion, and yet she turns him down. She can perceptively see through the Doctor's god complex and is not the type to be given over to blind or irrational faith. It is not immediately apparent then that her faith is stuck like the others at the conservative stage, or that she would therefore be digestible to the Minotaur. And yet when faced with her deepest fear, rejection and judgement by her harsh father, she falls back on the basics of her inherited faith. The prison, she reasons, is Jahannam, even if she is quite open to reinterpreting the tradition in the light of her present situation. The more logical conclusion, that the hotel was of an alien origin, should have been staring her in the face with the presence of Gibbis, whom she has already accepted as an alien[188].

The experience of being in the prison and the vision of her mocking father have brought about a regression in Rita's faith to the point that she has become delusional. Echoes of a more mature understanding remain, but her faith has become pathological, blind to its inherent contradictions. No longer a creative, affirming force, it is driven by a desire for death instead of life. This glorification of death is a constant feature, a sure indication that the Minotaur's food is cooked:

'...and soon he shall feast!'

[Joe]

'This is what happened to the others, and how lucky they were.'

[Lucy]

'He's going to kill us all. How cool is that?'

[Howie]

'Bring me death! Bring me glory! My master, my lord, I'm here! Come to me. I'm waiting here for you. He has promised me a glorious death. Give it to me now.'

---

[188] 'I'm going to file that under "freak out about later".'

[Howie]

'I'm not frightened. I'm blessed, Doctor.'

[Rita]

The courage and faith in which they each face their death, coupled with the explicitly religious language used, calls to mind the idolisation of religious martyrs within their own traditions. But there are significant differences. Religious and political martyrs are murdered for standing up for their convictions and refusing to acquiesce to another faith system or renounce a political allegiance. Death comes usually without any active desire to be killed on their part. By contrast, the victims of the God Complex abandon their faith and welcome death.

In the real world, martyrdom has taken on a greater symbolic significance, serving to support the ideological narratives of a religion by demonising opponents, glorifying subservience and encouraging belief in the afterlife. For instance in the Christian tradition, the numbers of martyrs are significantly exaggerated and the fact that it is more often than not Christians killing Christians is conveniently overlooked, with the evidence twisted to condemn Muslims among others[189]. It is almost as if a religion needs its martyrs to assert itself against competing traditions. Such extremism has brought about the horror of enforced renunciations and public executions. But again, none of these are particularly relevant to the deaths in *The God Complex*.

---

[189] Alexander, Ruth, 'Are There Really 100,000 New Christian Martyrs Every Year?'.

112

The prison is just drifting in space, and the deaths serve no greater end, whether as an example or a warning to others. In the original Minotaur myth, the sacrifices serve as a symbol of the Athenians' subservience to Crete. In *1984* the torture chambers are meant to install belief in Big Brother. Here the whole set up seems meaningless. None of the victims die with any expectation of an afterlife (for Rita, it will take her **out** of Jahannam), and death is not seen as a transition, but the end. They seem all to be aware that they will lose their individual identities and become food for the Minotaur. Gibbis worships subservience, but for him, death has no symbolic significance in that respect and crucially he is indigestible. And whilst they all change allegiances to worship the Minotaur, none of them demonise their past traditions in the process. Rita even has the presence of mind to ask the Doctor to remember her as she was, and she is able to say with no sense of anger or regret towards her tradition, 'Let me be robbed of my faith in private.'

The only other possible real world equivalent to *The God Complex* deaths brings us to the thorny subject of suicide bombers and others who actively seek to die for their cause. It is often assumed that the suicide bomber has been radicalised and brainwashed by religious extremists, but a comprehensive study by Robert Pape shows that 'there is far less of a connection between suicide terrorism and religious fundamentalism than most people think.' Instead, 'nearly all suicide terrorist attacks actually have in common [...] a specific secular and strategic goal''[190]

---

[190] Pape, Robert, 'Blowing Up an Assumption'.

It is still a matter of faith and conviction, even if not primarily a religious one. The suicide bomber is dying for a cause he or she identifies with. Whether or not they are religiously motivated or believe in an afterlife, they hope that their actions will trigger a change in the policies of their own governments and others. For many of them the logic of the greater good mitigates against the atrocities they are about to unleash. But in what sense can the worship of the Minotaur be a cause? Rita is determined to ensure that nobody else dies in the process, and there is of course no suggestion that she expects her death to be salvific for others.

In the same way that we try to make sense of the suicide bomber's mindset by claiming he or she must have been brainwashed or possessed, so too, the Doctor initially suspects that the victims of the prison are under some form of mental control or even possession. When he first sees Joe, his first question is 'Is Joe there?' The Doctor has seen enough examples of alien possession to suspect that Joe's bizarre behaviour and demeanour might signal that he is a puppet, just like the ventriloquists' dummies around him. The Tourette's-like involuntary 'Praise him' would appear to back up his theory, suggesting that the new religion is not a natural conversion during a journey through the stages of faith. But the Doctor is wrong in his assessment. However automatic their responses might seem, they are not alien. The new faith is pathological and not the result of alien takeover.

Whilst suicide bombers can show reasoning behind their actions, there is also evidence to suggest that a predisposing mental illness has determined what kind of terrorist they become. Adam Langford has made a convincing case that a higher than average number of suicide bombers already had suicidal tendencies or suffered from other psychological conditions[191]. Previous scholars had claimed that irrational, unwell individuals would be a liability to terrorist cells, but such conclusions assume that mental illness is easily detectable, labelling the depressed and suicidal as part of the lunatic fringe, the fools on the hill who are socially abnormal. A relationship between religion and mental illness can be subtle and private. In the case of Islamic suicide bombers (as an example) since suicide is a sin, but martyrdom a virtue, the latter might appeal to those yearning for the former[192].

Religion can provide an important support network to those suffering from fear and anxiety, and to those with more extreme conditions it might provide a positive narrative for understanding and interpreting them. In *The God Complex*, a case could be made for all the victims already having identity issues, such as depression, paranoia and psychosis, however well controlled. Amy has spent time in counselling because of her imaginary friend, but also her isolation and lack of parental figures. Howie has also been in therapy for his stammer. Joe claims that he is being forgiven for his inconstancy, which most likely relates to aborted efforts to kick his gambling addiction. With the forced exposure to fears, the alien environment, the separation from normality, and the threat of the Minotaur who represents the hidden monstrous within us all, there is no need for any superpower or alien agency to bring out these psychological predispositions. They have been fast-tracked by the extreme situation, making their appearance come across as

---

[191] Lankford, Adam, 'Martyr Myth: Inside the Minds of Suicide Bombers'.
[192] Lankford, 'Martyr Myth'.

possession. Joe, Howie and Lucy all show tell-tale physical signs of madness overcoming them, but just because Rita appears to be in control, this need not mean that she was not also suffering from depression or another psychological condition, perhaps triggered by her need to find approval.

A Survival Mechanism

We have seen how religion is a form of control for the builders of the prison and a symptom of mental illness for its victims. But what of the prisoner? For the Minotaur, the pathological religiosity of others is critical to its survival. Without a constant supply of faith, the creature will die. But what, if anything, does the Minotaur believe in? There is precious little to go on. Despite being central to the story, we only hear three lines from the Minotaur, all roughly translated by the Doctor:

> 'Did you say "they take"? Ah, what is that word? "The guard"? No, "the warden"? This is a prison.'

> 'So what are we, cell mates? Lunch? "We are not ripe." This is what Joe said, that we weren't ready. So, what, what, you make us ready. You what? "Replace"? Replace what, fear? "You have lived so long even your name is lost. You want this to stop. Because you are just instinct." Then tell me. Tell me how to fight you.'

> '"An ancient creature, drenched in the blood of the innocent, drifting in space through an endless, shifting maze. For such a creature, death would be a gift." Then accept it, and sleep well. "I wasn't talking about myself."'

The first is to explain the setting and the fact that he is a prisoner, the second to express his desire to be freed, and the third turns out to be a statement about the Doctor. It is not until the final sentence that the Doctor has got the hang of interpreting its words, and so the only statements we have about its condition are broken and unreliable. The Doctor even misreads his own theory onto the creature's lips. Significantly the creature no longer has a name, at least not when it is hungry. The Minotaur's remote prison wardens have turned its own weapon against itself. The faith that had once kept them submissive and was presumably metaphorically fed to them by the Minotaur, and quite possibly other members of its species, is now seemingly being used to feed **it**. But if the Minotaur has no independent existence, is it therefore, literally only alive because people still believe in it?

The only thing that we can be sure the Minotaur believes in is that its existence is so meaningless it would be better off dead. That belief is projected not only onto the Doctor, but onto all its victims, and so it kills them instead of accepting their worship. Their faith, expressed as worship, is taken by the Minotaur to reinforce his own paradoxical faith in death. They only want to die because he does. They are not literally a food source; it doesn't find physical nourishment from their bodies, but leaves them behind as an empty shell. Where exactly all that rotting flesh is remains a mystery; perhaps they are jettisoned or, more chillingly, used as food sources for other victims. But if the feeding is not literal, then how is the Minotaur still alive at all without a physical food source?

One possible answer is that the life-support system of the ship is keeping its prisoner alive, whether through temporal engineering, constricting a thousand years into a day, or through some kind of

117

chemical process in the atmosphere. The Minotaur wants nothing more than for one of its potential victims to play the role of Theseus and destroy it, yet the ship makes this impossible.

It would be a mistake to assume the creature dies because its food source has been taken away from it by the Doctor breaking Amy's faith. That would turn a metaphor into a literal feeding. What changes, what kills the Minotaur, is the ship reverting back to its basic form. The ship changes before the creature dies, not the other way around. The creature would probably have died years ago, were it not for the artificial and temporally anomalous environment. The ship itself needed the fears and faiths of others to sustain itself. Perhaps, at first, it worked when the creature still believed in its own divinity, but once it had lost faith and paradoxically yearned for death, all the ship had left to keep its engines running were the fears and faiths of those it brought on board. Amy's faith was by this point its last bit of fuel.

Faith according to this interpretation is a survival mechanism, not for the Minotaur, nor even for its victims, but for the ship itself. Neither the God, nor his worshippers, but the system that sustained them was completely dependent on faith. It is not the gods of religion who require worship, but the religions themselves. If the gods were real then they would still exist even if nobody believed in them. And without an inherited religion to fall back on, the will to live would express itself in other forms of faith. The universal collapse of belief, especially in its conservative phase, would mean the end of religious institutions. They would be exposed as an artificial construct, just like the 80s hotel in space.

THE FALLIBLE HERO

Since the character came back to our screens in 2005, questions surrounding the identity of the Doctor have played a central role. Putting a question mark at the end of 'Doctor Who' is hardly revolutionary, of course. It is a theme that bookends the 20th-century series, with the 1987-89 script editor Andrew Cartmel restoring some of that foundational mystery behind the character, which had gradually been eroded through over familiarity. There is an essential unknowability about the Doctor that needs to be preserved to keep the legend alive[193]. On those rare occasions when specific answers are given, they tend to be controversial, insofar as they limit the possibilities by being too definitive[194].

Asking questions **of** the Doctor by challenging his morality, heroism and effectiveness is also not particularly new[195]. The Doctor resists basking in the limelight, but his diffidence is characterised more as humility than true self-doubt, calling to mind the 'messianic secret'

---

[193] Unused drafts of Antony Coburn's *An Unearthly Child* (1963) contained explicit statements about the Doctor and Susan's background, causing David Whitaker to comment: 'I think it ought to be done in a lighter way.' Two drafts later, all references to their background had gone. For a detailed study of each version of the script, see Bignell, Richard, 'An Unearthly Beginning', DWM #467.
[194] *The Deadly Assassin* (1976) and *Doctor Who* (1996) were particular targets for criticism.
[195] See especially *The War Games* (1969) and *The Trial Of A Time Lord* (1986).

of Mark's gospel[196], as this closing scene from *The Web of Fear* (1968) aptly illustrates:

ANNE

You were a hero, and you know it.

DOCTOR

You don't really think so, do you?

ANNE

Yes, yes, I do.

CHORLEY

You've got to face facts, old man. By tomorrow morning you're going to be a household word, a national figure.

DOCTOR

Oh, no. Oh, no.

CHORLEY

Yes. I want you on my television programme, and...

---

[196] This theory was originally put forward by William Wrede as an ancient way of accounting for the disparity between history and belief about Jesus' identity as Messiah. Subsequently, numerous other scholarly explanations have been proposed for Jesus' secrecy in the gospel, and the body of literature is vast. But it is interesting to note the similarities with Odysseus, which may or may not have been intentional on the gospel writer's part. Others suggest that the secret is a consequence of his humility (Bazzell, Pascal D, *Urban Ecclesiology* (2015), p130).

DOCTOR

Oh, no!

CHORLEY

And I want to organise a big press conference, and...

DOCTOR

Jamie! Victoria! Come along, it's time we left.

What sets apart the revived series is that the Doctor is finally moved to properly question himself, culminating in a total rejection of the notion that he is a hero. His role in the Time War triggers this self-critical, tragic consciousness. Thereafter, for the most part he fights against his powers in an effort to redeem himself. Nonetheless, there are times when he gives in to the inherent dangers of his godlike status. He no longer assumes the moral high ground in every situation. Time and time again he finds himself being called to account, by both enemies and friends.

There is now an ambiguity inherent in the Doctor's heroic status, which is best encapsulated by the impact his actions have upon his companions. It's not just that some of them will occasionally end up as martyrs, like Adric[197]. The consequences that their involvement with the Doctor have upon their worlds are now shown to affect every aspect, including careers and relationships. The treatment of Sarah Jane, who crosses both eras of the show, well illustrates this change[198]. Originally, the only negative side of

---

[197] *Earthshock.*

[198] See also the return in **The Sarah Jane Adventures**: *Death of the Doctor* (2010) of Jo Grant, who left in *The Green Death* (1973) with

her departure from the Doctor is that she is inconveniently dropped off in the wrong place[199]. It can be laughed off and quickly rectified. But in **The Sarah Jane Adventures** we see that the consequence of her time with the Doctor is her inability to form relationships. The impact is deeply personal and lasting. Another indication of this shift in storytelling can be found by comparing the departure of Zoe and Jamie with Donna Noble's[200]. They are all returned to their lives as if they had never left with the Doctor. For Zoe and Jamie the audience is not in any way led to consider the consequences, yet for Donna we clearly are.

Series six ratchets up just how much of a mess the Doctor can make of people's lives, with the story of Amy's kidnapped baby. His farewell gift of a home and car provides scant compensation for the cost of their discipleship and calls to mind the 10th Doctor's lottery ticket numbers for Donna[201]. In this context, the Minotaur's words for the Doctor carry a deeper resonance than, say, Davros's taunts in *Journey's End* (2008). The Doctor's vulnerability and guilt lie hidden behind a superficial 'one of the lads' persona, a self-defining heroism, a manic quest for adventures and a quick-fix strategy. All four are forms of escape and denial, turning him into a parody of his former self. It is the 11th Doctor trying to be the 10th Doctor, and consequently comes across as false. The 10th Doctor, the one who didn't want to go, is very much still present. And so the

---

remarkable ease, yet now we discover it was not quite so straightforward adjusting to life without the Doctor: 'Sometimes I think I've never stopped running.'
[199] *The Hand Of Fear* (1976).
[200] *The War Games, Journey's End* (2008).
[201] *The End of Time* part 2.

starkest, boldest criticism ever made of the Doctor – that he would be better off dead – breaks the latent desire for immortality that hangs over him from his former incarnation. This is the harshest deconstruction of the Doctor's heroism to date, because unlike the 12th Doctor's musings on whether or not he is a good man[202], the stakes are much higher. If the Doctor has lost faith in himself, this could be the end. We know the Doctor dies on Lake Silencio, and are forced to ask whether or not he will want to avoid such a fate.

What Kind Of Hero Is The Doctor?

To understand just how far *The God Complex* deconstructs the Doctor, we need to consider what kind of hero he is in the first place. The Doctor is certainly not an anti-hero, in the same league as, say, Malcolm Reynolds or Kerr Avon, who lack conventional heroic attributes[203]. But neither is he a superhero in the traditional sense of an individual endowed with extraordinary powers and technology, driven by an absolute commitment to a cause. Instead, he displays characteristics of both extremes. His superhero mantra, 'neither cruel or cowardly,'[204] almost defines him, but on occasions he spectacularly fails to practice what he preaches. The closest the Doctor gets to being an anti-hero is in his War Doctor incarnation, which so goes against his heroic sensibilities that he refuses to refer

---

[202] *Into the Dalek* (2014).

[203] In **Firefly** and **Blake's 7** respectively.

[204] *The Day of the Doctor*, taken from a Terrance Dicks quote that appeared in the *Radio Times* 10th anniversary Special in 1973. Later the 12th Doctor qualifies the description, another indication that, for now at least, he has been stripped of his god complex: 'Never be cruel and never be cowardly. And if you ever are, always make amends.' (*Hell Bent* (2015)).

to this incarnation as the Doctor. It remains a complete aberration, to the extent that he considers the anti-hero to be the anti-Doctor, even after the existential changes brought about in *The God Complex*. Despite this, the War Doctor is never driven by the characteristic self-interest of the anti-hero who can be good and bad, in both actions **and** motivations.

The Doctor as a hero is motivated by a commitment to justice. Like countless superheroes, however, that persuasion lacks the human element of compassion to undergird it. He acts out of duty more than love, and can therefore appear cold and calculating, or unmoved by suffering[205]. Towards the end of his 10th incarnation, he has fully embraced that superhero consciousness, moving from the hapless Arthur Dent[206] image of *The Christmas Invasion* (2005) and losing his hand in the process, to the benevolent god, watching from afar and bestowing blessings and salvation on his friends, in *The End of Time* part 2.

As soon as we delve more deeply into the nature of the superhero, it becomes clear that the Doctor is not so different from them after all. The cross-fertilisation of comic books, movies, novels and TV series has led to a blurring of the boundary between the ordinary hero and the superhero. The Doctor is the perfect example, with comic-book writers such as Paul Cornell and Neil Gaiman

---

[205] Roman Altshuler uses the different term 'concern' to contrast the Doctor's ethics with human compassion, which allows for impartiality ('Is the Doctor the destroyer of Worlds?' in Lewis, Courtland, and Paula Smithka, eds, *Doctor Who and Philosophy* (2010), p292).
[206] In Douglas Adams' **The Hitchhiker's Guide to the Galaxy**.

contributing scripts. He is the British equivalent of **Buffy the Vampire Slayer** (1997-2003). Both characters are a fusion of the action hero with the superhero. Danny Fingeroth defines this cross-pollination as the superhero comic-consciousness, 'by which I mean the hope (and fear) that there may be more to this world than what we see.'[207] Seemingly ordinary things are frequently given a higher significance in **Doctor Who**, whether they be shadows (*Silence in the Library / Forest of the Dead* (2008)), statues (*Blink* (2007)), graffiti (*Flatline*), or monsters hiding under the bed (*Listen* (2014)). One of the Doctor's core roles is to tune us in to this alternative way of looking at the everyday, bringing the extraordinary into the ordinary.

Like the superhero with an often dual identity, the Doctor also enables us to see ourselves differently, bringing us into a liminal state between various opposites[208], such as material and spiritual, good and evil, belonging and alienation, impotence and power, and instinct and control. He might not wear a mask or costume, and only occasionally use the John Smith card, but the very concept of regeneration suggests that his face and body themselves fulfil those functions. His distinctive clothing sets him apart physically, to signal the fact that he lives on the cusp between belonging and not-belonging. The 11th Doctor's bow-tie, which he unfashionably describes as cool, is more than a signifier of a quirky dress sense. It

---

[207] Fingeroth, Danny, *Superman on the Couch* (2004), p29.

[208] Roz Kaveney describes the superhero's dual identity as a liminal state (*Superheroes! Capes and Crusaders in Comics and Films* (2007), p5). For a fuller treatment of this feature, see Fingeroth, *Superman on the Couch*, pp49ff.

is the unrealistic, over the top attempt to both hide and reveal, fit in and stand out: the equivalent of Clark Kent's glasses.

The Doctor is not far from being a superhero in the more generalised sense. His powers are both inherently superior and enhanced through alien technology. He is orphaned and cut off, not only from his family, but from his whole race. He both belongs and does not belong. He gathers around him various sidekicks. He has an ambivalent relationship with the authorities. He has a shadow side (compare the Dream Lord with Bizarro, or the Valeyard with Venom[209]). But there are two significant differences. He rarely resorts to violence, the virtually universal primary mode of the superhero's engagement with evil[210], but neither does he share their almost religious moral superiority[211].

Perhaps the most helpful model for unpacking what kind of hero the Doctor is, comes from the field of psychology and Carl Jung's hero archetype[212]. Campbell used Jung's subcategories to plot the hero's journey as an underlying structure behind most works of fiction. For Jung, the hero is a paradoxical figure: 'human but raised to the limit of the supernatural, he is semi-divine.'[213] The hero's

---

[209] The Dream Lord appeared in *Amy's Choice*, and the Valeyard in *The Trial of a Time Lord*. Bizarro and Venom are antagonists and doubles of Superman and Spider-Man respectively.

[210] For a discussion of the superhero's primary mode of engagement as violent, see Kaveney, *Superheroes!*, pp12ff.

[211] Ben Saunders, for instance, sees a religious quality to Superman's selflessness (*Do the Gods Wear Capes?* (2011), p32).

[212] See for example, Dominiguez-Cheo, Amanda, '**Doctor Who**: A Hero's Journey'.

[213] Jung, CG, *Essays on a Science of Mythology* (1949), p85.

story is the externalisation of the struggle between the conscious and unconscious, or between control and instinct. The beasts without, whether dragons, giants or minotaurs, are projections of the demons within: 'The hero's main feat is to overcome the monster of darkness.'[214] Once overcome, he is able to acquire the treasure, whether it be a ring, a princess, or the elixir of life. When the beast is defeated, the hero typically returns home to be crowned as a saviour figure.

Such a pattern is clearly broken in *The God Complex*, for whilst the Minotaur is defeated, what has the Doctor achieved? The gifts he brings to Amy and Rory at the end are not dependent on slaying the Minotaur, and his victory comes not from any superior power, knowledge, or technology[215], but from deliberately breaking the illusion of his semi-divinity. It's as if the Doctor has to artificially complete the hero's story, by finding replacement or compensatory gifts. The episode ends with a haunting shot of the Doctor alone in the TARDIS again; there is no victory parade, or even a message of thanks. In Jung's analysis the hero's rewards are illustrative of finding one's true feelings and potential. His task is to make whole, by bringing the conscious and unconscious together. The lack of resolution here, the awkward and artificial way in which the story ends, means that this feeling of wholeness cannot be achieved. The shadow of death and darkness, instead of being defeated, looms larger than ever.

---

[214] Jung, CG, *Collected Works*, 9.1 paragraph 284.
[215] Notice how the TARDIS has disappeared and the sonic screwdriver hurts the Doctor's ears.

The God Complex has exposed us to our nightmare rooms, confronted us with the Minotaur as a representation of our untameable instincts and shadow selves, only to cast us aside, like Rory and Amy, with nothing but material things to make us feel better. And to make matters worse the Doctor has placed a 'Do Not Disturb' sign on his own door, as if part of his god complex is the assumption that he can let out and overcome other people's fears, whilst denying his own. Instead of being a wounded healer, he expects or demands of himself that he be an immutable God.

Using the metaphor of a journey, Campbell describes how the hero passes through several stages, and may or may not fall in the process. For instance at one stage he can either use his powers like a benevolent ruler or an oppressive tyrant[216]. The Doctor has demonstrated both extremes: aware that his powers can be abused for the greater good, he can display a lack of mercy and compassion that shocks his companions[217]. He is cursed by the constant dilemma of the reluctant hero, one with which his arch-nemesis, Missy, confronts him in *Death In Heaven* (2014), when she offers him the Cybermen army:

> 'Well, I don't need one, do I? Armies are for people who think they're right. And nobody thinks they're righter than you. Give a good man firepower, and he'll never run out of people to kill.'

---

[216] Campbell, Joseph, *The Hero with a Thousand Faces* (1949), pp319-322.
[217] See for example, Amy (*A Town Called Mercy*), and Donna (*The Runaway Bride*, 2006).

Jung theorises that individuals can develop pathological hero complexes, where they set themselves up as saviour figures and find it virtually impossible to say 'No' to people who claim to be in need. The 10th Doctor says that 'Help me' are two words he can never refuse[218]. An even more extreme version of this illusionary altruistic mindset is the Messiah complex. Such people make grandiose claims about their ability to save a whole society, if not the world. But though he is on the hero's journey, the Doctor occasionally shirks away from exercising such responsibility, whether through indecision[219], cowardice[220], self-interest[221], or sheer bloody-mindedness[222]. Such exceptions suggest that the Messiah complex that drove the 10th Doctor to change a fixed point in time in *The Waters Of Mars* (2009), is not atypical, but is something he has always wrestled with. His self-identification as the Doctor shows that he sets himself up as the saviour figure.

The 11th Doctor rejects any moralistic notion that he is a good man. His mission to save is therefore not born out of some essential goodness. Like many superheroes[223], personal tragedy and loss lie behind his heroism. That defining experience of losing Gallifrey is played out again and again vicariously, intensifying through his relationship with his chosen companions. We have seen how duty rather than compassion governs his thinking, but when it comes to the social network he gathers around him, he can

---

[218] *The Next Doctor* (2008).
[219] *Genesis Of The Daleks* (1975).
[220] *Resurrection Of The Daleks* (1984).
[221] Refusing the presidency in *The Five Doctors* (1983).
[222] *Kill the Moon* (2014).
[223] E.g. Batman and Superman.

also be motivated by powerful emotions of love and anger, surprising himself in the process.

DOCTOR

I want people to call you Colonel Run-Away. I want children laughing outside your door, because they've found the house of Colonel Run-Away. And, when people come to you, and ask if trying to get to me through the people I love is in any way a good idea, I want you to tell them your name. Oh, look, I'm angry. That's new. I'm really not sure what's going to happen now.

KOVARIAN

The anger of a good man is not a problem. Good men have too many rules.

DOCTOR

Good men don't need rules. Today is not the day to find out why I have so many.[224]

Compassion is later seen as the Doctor's weakness by Davros, which at first glance contradicts the notion that the Doctor is governed by duty rather than empathy:

DOCTOR

There's no such thing as the Doctor. I'm just a bloke in a box. Telling stories! And I didn't come here because I'm ashamed. A bit of shame never hurt anyone. I came...

---

[224] *A Good Man Goes to War.*

because you're sick and you asked. And because sometimes, on a good day, if I try very hard, I'm not some old Time Lord who ran away. I'm the Doctor.

DAVROS

Compassion then.

DOCTOR

Always.

DAVROS

It grows strong and fierce in you, like a cancer.

DOCTOR

I hope so.

DAVROS

It will kill you in the end.

DOCTOR

I wouldn't die of anything else.

DAVROS

You may rely on it.[225]

---

[225] *The Witch's Familiar* (2015). Note that the same observation is made by the Daleks in *Victory of the Daleks* (2010). However, the Doctor falls short of saving Bracewell, because the limits of his empathy mean he can only go so far in disarming the bomb. Amy is needed to step in to complete the task of drawing out Bracewell's humanity, by reminding him of his memories of a lover. In the same

And yet his friends (e.g. Donna, *The Runaway Bride*) call him out for lacking such a human quality. How can Davros and Donna both be right? The compassion of the Doctor is reactive, dependent on the sometimes unhealthy relationships he has formed to ward off loneliness. It is a compassion based on love and insecurity rather than empathy and goodness, and so is directed towards those he cares most about, those he feels guilty for, or those he sees himself in. Concern for his companions interferes with his Messiah complex, presenting dilemmas such as those many occasions in which he is forced to choose between saving a friend and saving the world, or the times when a friend asks him to break the rules for her (e.g. *Dark Water* (2015)). The Doctor knows it is a weakness (he doesn't class it as a superpower, like fear or forgetfulness), but it is one he is prepared to embrace because it is the only thing that prevents him from becoming all-powerful.

That the Doctor's consciousness as a hero is something he fights against, is perhaps best illustrated in *Amy's Choice* (2010), when the Dream Lord, representing the Doctor's hidden self, uses it to tempt Amy away from Rory:

> 'So what's his name? Now, which one of these men would you really choose? Look at them. You ran away with a handsome hero. Would you really give him up for a

---

story, the Doctor needs the prompting of the humans to reassure him that the freedom of the Daleks was a price worth paying for saving the earth. He also resists his hero complex in the story, pointing out to Winston Churchill that the earth does not need him, and that the British PM is set to become the hero.

bumbling country doctor who thinks the only thing he needs to be interesting is a ponytail?'

The hero complex is therefore part of the Doctor's shadow side. It can be manipulative and self-serving, blind to the suffering of others in its impulsiveness. The same mocking voice of the Dream Lord is used by the Doctor against Colonel Stanton, and is a regular feature whenever he appears to act without mercy. For the Doctor, being a hero is a liability that brings out the best and worst in him.

In series six, the Doctor is presented as a hero by others[226], and even though he maintains a certain ambivalence towards such a status, it is a role he is happy to assume. But by the middle of the next series he has seemingly abandoned his position. In *The Snowmen* (2012), Madame Vastra reveals:

VASTRA

The Doctor is not kind.

CLARA

No?

VASTRA

No. The Doctor doesn't help people. Not anyone, not ever. He stands above this world and doesn't interfere in the affairs of its inhabitants. He is not your salvation, nor your protector. Do you understand what I am saying to you?

---

[226] E.g. Octavian (*Flesh and Stone*), Lorna (*A Good Man Goes to War*).

CLARA

Words.

VASTRA

He was different once, a long time ago. Kind, yes. A hero,
even. A saviour of worlds. But he suffered losses which hurt
him. Now he prefers isolation to the possibility of pain's
return.

It's a very different state of affairs from the Doctor announcing
himself as the Earth's defender in the 11th Doctor's first story, *The
Eleventh Hour* (2010). The loss of Amy and Rory precipitated this
dereliction of duty[227], but the scales had already been lifted in *The
God Complex*. Instead of following the Minotaur's advice by
embracing death, he cheated it once again. The Doctor is acting
with the otherness and aloofness of a transcendent God who
watches over us without intervening, in contrast to an imminent
God who lives and breathes through his creation. His god complex
is not undone, merely redefined.

In a point so easily overlooked, the redemption of the War
Doctor[228] also brings a resolution to the incomplete deconstruction
of the Doctor as hero in *The God Complex*. Despite the Minotaur's
warning, the Doctor does not entirely give up on his Messianic
agenda. Even when he has finally reneged on his sense of duty, he
still cannot help looking down on the Earth from the clouds[229]. A

---

[227] *The Angels Take Manhattan* (2012).
[228] *The Day of the Doctor.*
[229] *The Snowmen.*

true withdrawal would see him find some secluded corner of the universe in which to meditate alone. But just as the War Doctor was 'Doctor no more'[230], the 11th Doctor was, in his own mind at least, hero no more. He has an identity crisis, and it takes Clara to bring his warring natures together:

CLARA

Look at you. The three of you. The warrior, the hero, and you.

[11TH] DOCTOR

And what am I?

CLARA

Have you really forgotten?

DOCTOR

Yes. Maybe, yes.

CLARA

We've got enough warriors. Any old idiot can be a hero.

DOCTOR

Then what do I do?

CLARA

What you've always done. Be a doctor.

---

[230] 'The Night of the Doctor'.

The War Doctor represents the beast, the shadow, while the 10th Doctor represents the hero fighting against it, and failing spectacularly[231]. Jung argued that the reason why Christianity has a history of violence, is because of this suppression of instinct[232]. The same theory would account for the atrocities committed by the Doctor as the 'destroyer of worlds'. The 11th Doctor is encouraged by Clara to be true to his self: to be neither a warrior, nor a hero, but a Doctor.

The Doctor, as a name, represents the coming together of the conscious and unconscious: he is not an alternative to the warrior and the hero, but their unification. A Doctor fights disease and a Doctor heals the sick. He is the warrior and hero in one[233]. In order to be effective, he has to embrace the fact that he is a wounded healer, that he needs to be healed himself. He must act like a hero without developing a Messiah complex, and act like a warrior without bringing death and destruction in his wake.

In *The God Complex*, the Doctor fails to be a doctor. The Minotaur is not healed. Lives are not saved. Instead of being true to himself, he entered the complex trying to be a hero, whilst denying the warrior inside him. His fractured self is in need of healing. When the less intense 11th Doctor took up the reins, we were led to assume that the regeneration had cleaned the slate. This was a new, youthful Doctor, freed from his predecessor's angst-ridden

---

[231] See *The Waters of Mars*.
[232] Jung, *Collected Works* 10.22.
[233] This thought lies behind the translation of Doctor as 'Great Warrior' by the people of the Gamma Forest (*A Good Man Goes to War*).

Messiah complex. But the transition was not a conversion experience. There is far less difference between the two sides of this particular regeneration, than in any other. He has not been born again, and yet he lives under the illusion that he can tame the excesses of his previous self. The Minotaur's devastating last words bring to him the realisation that he is no different after all.

According to Steven Moffat:

> 'A hero isn't someone who's built by nature to be a hero [...] it's someone who conquers their own weaknesses when they need to.'[234]

Ironically, the Doctor's weakness is that by nature he is superhuman and expects therefore to be a Messiah figure. It is a weakness known only too well by his enemies and friends alike:

> 'From what I've seen, your funny little happy-go-lucky life leaves devastation in its wake; always moving on because you dare not look back. Playing with so many people's lives, you might as well be a god.'

> [Margaret the Slitheen, *Boom Town* (2005)]

> 'Why is it up to you to save us? That's quite a god complex you have there.'

> [Rita, *The God Complex*]

Elsewhere Moffat, in comparing the Doctor to Sherlock Holmes, suggests that he is an angel wanting to be a man[235]. The Doctor's

---

[234] Moffat, Steven, and Peter Capaldi, 'The Doctor: A Different Kind of Hero'.

heroic journey is to set aside, limit, or control those innate powers in order to embrace a humanist agenda. It would explain why his chosen companions are almost always humans. In that respect, the exposure of his god complex is a positive and necessary step in that journey. He needs to be moved from the tyrant/ruler stage of the hero's quest, to that of the redeemer.

According to Campbell, 'The hero of yesterday becomes the tyrant of tomorrow, unless he crucifies **himself** today.'[236] For the 11th Doctor this ought to have meant succumbing to his fate at Lake Silencio, but instead he gets a reprieve, not because of the salvific actions of his friends, but because of his own cleverness. The climax of the series neatly contrasts with the Doctor's ultimate Messianic act in the previous season's finale, *The Big Bang* (2010). This time, the audience is expecting his followers to be gathering to save **him**:

> 'The sky is full of a million million voices saying yes, of course we'll help. You've touched so many lives, saved so many people. Did you think when your time came, you'd really have to do more than just ask? You've decided that the universe is better off without you, but the universe doesn't agree.'

> [River Song, *The Wedding Of River Song* (2011)].

For a few moments, we are misdirected into assuming that the Doctor has indeed taken on board the words of the Minotaur, and that it will be down to his friends to save him. The Doctor makes

---

[235] See Ashir-Perrin, Emily, '**Doctor Who** 4/12 NYC Premiere Screening Q & A Transcript!'.
[236] Campbell, *The Hero with a Thousand Faces*, p326.

the same mistaken conclusion, horrified that his friends are prepared to sacrifice billions of lives in order to save him. River has to correct his assumption:

RIVER

I can't let you die.

DOCTOR

But I have to die.

RIVER:

Shut up! I can't let you die without knowing you are loved by so many, and so much, and by no one more than me.

Only a person with a god complex could expect such undying devotion from his followers. The Doctor pulls one more trick out of his sleeve, fooling everyone, including the viewers, by saving himself using the Teselecta[237]. The events of *The God Complex* are therefore only a partial redemption. At the most, the Minotaur has simply made him aware of his flaws.

The story of the 11th Doctor continues to be played out as his journey towards the inevitability of death, bringing him to Trenzalore where he makes his final stand[238]. Fully accepting his mortality, now he embraces the warrior and hero within. This time, when the possibility of his salvation presents itself, it does indeed

---

[237] A plan he had set in motion before finding out that River was prepared to die with him.
[238] *The Time of the Doctor.*

come from his friends, with Clara gaining the help of the Time Lords in granting the Doctor a new regeneration cycle.

It is in this, his final story, that the contents of Room 11 from *The God Complex* are revealed. At first glance it might seem to be a little out of place; an unnecessary retcon, twisting the scene so that it fits into wider arc of the Matt Smith years. The fact that the Doctor says 'Who else?' and yet we are now supposed to believe that the room contained the crack in time, seems to highlight how forced this reading is. But it is no coincidence that the door to Room 11 is finally opened to the viewers at the point in which the Doctor has taken on board the Minotaur's example; accepting death, and freeing himself of the god complex. The call-back is a quite deliberate signal that *The God Complex* foreshadows *The Time of the Doctor*.

Speculation as to what constituted the Doctor's greatest fear was the major talking point following the original broadcast of *The God Complex*. Whithouse had his own ideas about the contents of Room 11, but never revealed them, preferring to leave the door closed and the question open. But it is not immediately apparent why the crack in time should be his greatest fear. Perhaps it is a conditioned response, the symbol that triggers a greater fear. After all, the Doctor seemed curious about the crack at first. The Doctor claims that the only way to close one of the time-space fissures is to feed it with a complicated time-space event, such as the Weeping Angels or himself. It might therefore call to mind the primal fear of death. But more specifically, since the crack is caused by the TARDIS's explosion, perhaps the loss of the TARDIS is in view.

The TARDIS is referred to by the Doctor as a person, making sense of the 'who else' line. And it would explain the sound of the cloister bell emitting from the room in *The God Complex*. The destruction of the TARDIS would be the ultimate loss for the Doctor; loss of his closest companion, but also loss of his freedom to travel across time and space on his Messianic, super-heroic quests.

The Doctor's first face in his new regenerative cycle continues to reflect on his heroic status[239]. He starts out denying that he is a hero, despite Clara's protestations. The hero's quest is starting from scratch again. In the same way that the 11th Doctor is dealing with the unresolved issues of his predecessor, so too the 12th Doctor continues where his former self left off. In Mark Gatiss' *Robot Of Sherwood* (2014), when Clara is trying to point out that he is in fact a hero[240], he sips custard from a spoon, reminding the viewer of the 11th Doctor. Later, once again when the subject of his heroism comes up[241], Matt Smith's Doctor is not far from view, as the Doctor tastes an apple just as he did in *The God Complex*. It is not the only link to *The God Complex* in the episode, for once again the Doctor hears some poignant words about himself that he assumes relate to the speaker:

---

[239] *The Girl Who Died* (2015).
[240] 'You stop bad things happening every minute of every day. That sounds pretty heroic to me.'
[241] 'When did you start believing in impossible heroes?' (the Doctor to Clara).

141

ROBIN

Is it so hard to credit? That a man born into wealth and privilege should find the plight of the oppressed and weak too much to bear...

DOCTOR

No.

ROBIN

Until one night he is moved to steal a TARDIS? Fly among the stars, fighting the good fight. Clara told me your stories.

DOCTOR

She should not have told you any of that.

ROBIN

Well. Well, once the story started, she could hardly stop herself. You are her hero, I think.

DOCTOR

I'm not a hero.

ROBIN

Well, neither am I. But if we both keep pretending to be. Ha-ha! Perhaps others will be heroes in our name. Perhaps we will both be stories. And may those stories never end.

Later in the series finale, *Death in Heaven*, the Doctor, recalls this very conversation when, echoing the 11th Doctor's words in *The God Complex*, he tells Missy:

'I am not a good man! I am not a bad man. I am not a hero. And I'm definitely not a president. And no, I'm not an officer. Do you know what I am? I am an idiot, with a box and a screwdriver. Just passing through, helping out, learning. I don't need an army. I never have, because I've got them. Always them. Because love, it's not an emotion. Love is a promise.'

The idea of love as commitment brings together compassion and compulsion, the hero and the warrior, the man and the beast, the conscious and the unconscious. It is, to use the terminology of Jung, the individuation that frees the Doctor from his god complex.

We have spoken about the stages of faith in relation to others brought into the god complex. But what of the Doctor's own faith? He evades the question 'What do time lords pray to?' not because it is irrelevant but precisely because it is fundamental, relevant and important. The Doctor's faith is inherently secular; there is no role in it for Gallifreyan gods or legendary figures. But it would be wrong to place a false dichotomy between faith and science, or magic and technology.

Over time the Doctor's faith still manifests itself in all its different stages, including the conservative. It is beyond the scope of this study to chart the various movements in his faith journey, but suffice to say that what links the faith of the Doctor to religious beliefs is the place of story. Certain principles arise out of the Doctor's core narrative, which become more or less important and mutable; at times they are dogmatic assertions, at others guiding principles, occasionally they might even be deconstructed, but the overarching stimulus behind them remains constant. For the

Doctor, story is everything. It fires imagination, creativity and opportunity. The self-awareness that we are continually writing stories as a way of making sense of the world and our place within it, is very much a postmodern mindset, but it need not be reduced to a relativistic, 'anything goes' impotence. For as the Doctor says to Amy, 'We are all stories in the end. Just make it a good one.'[242]

The Doctor knows that stories are constructs, and that the hero himself is one such invention. After all, he comes from a race who can use the Matrix technology to turn false testimony into historical truth. The labels of hero and villain must serve to protect the status quo on Gallifrey. In the false ending of *The Deadly Assassin* (1977), Borusa attempts to sanitise the preceding events, fabricating the truth and turning the assassin Goth into a martyr:

BORUSA

Our story is going to be that the Master arrived in Gallifrey to assassinate the President, secretly. Before he could escape, Chancellor Goth tracked him down and killed him, unfortunately perishing himself in the exchange of fire. Now that's much better. I can believe that.

ENGIN

You're making Goth into a hero?

BORUSA

If heroes don't exist, it is necessary to invent them. Good for public morale.

---

[242] *The Big Bang.*

Borusa's interference with the Matrix records does not end there: in order for Goth to become the unequivocal hero, the Doctor's role in the affair is to be erased, and the Master's villainy accentuated. Borusa asks the Doctor to help Engin to prepare a biog for the Master that will make his nemesis a 'public enemy', advising him 'it doesn't have to be entirely accurate'.

Later, the Doctor parodies this *1984* style rewriting of history by his own people[243], but it is not at all clear whether or not he would have been complicit in twisting the truth in his testimony about the Master. After all, he confesses to Spandrell that he hopes the Master did not survive, adding 'and there's no one in all the galaxies I'd say that about. The quintessence of evil.'[244] It seems that the Doctor needs heroes and villains as much as the rest of us[245]. The Doctor, the true hero in that story, has to be written out of the history book, because he is an unconventional maverick, the antithesis of a hero of the state. He is more than happy to oblige. He is always the people's hero, and never a puppet of the establishment, even when he finds himself on the payroll. That said, it is important not to idealise or romanticise this notion of the Doctor as the people's champion. Even if that is his orientation, according to Steven Moffat's vision of the character, he is not always best placed to bring it about, given his aristocratic background. In a deleted scene from *Hell Bent* (2015), the Doctor

---

[243] 'Well, you'll just have to adjust the truth again, Cardinal. What about subsidence owing to a plague of mice?'
[244] *The Deadly Assassin* episode 4.
[245] Though at times his choice of hero is questionable – e.g. Omega (*The Three Doctors* (1972-73)), Salyavin (*Shada* (1979, unbroadcast)).

tells Ohila that he has re-employed the members of the High Council as sewer workers. Ohila points out to him that only a person of privileged status could regard such work as punishment. Moffat comments:

> '...he knows that the aristocracy must be deposed, but even in bringing it about, he reveals that he will always be one of them. If he's any kind of role model, it's because he tries to be good, not because he already is.'

The ramifications of *The God Complex* upon the Doctor's self-understanding, position him in agreement with Moffat's deconstructed hero. The Messianic undertones of Russell T Davies's lonely god are worlds apart from Moffat's characterisation, and for continuity's sake require story-driven triggers to bring the viewers in line with his thinking. For Steven Moffat, the Doctor's god/hero/messiah complex is his biggest downfall: 'Every character failing [the Doctor] has is based on his assumption that he is cleverer, and more important, and more entitled than everyone else in the room.'[246]

The Doctor frequently makes it his business to deconstruct other heroes and villains, challenging such labels, whether of their own making or others, in order to effect change where necessary. At his best he encourages those who see themselves as insignificant to realise their heroic potential (e.g. Gwyneth[247], the Thals[248]), whilst lampooning those who think too highly of themselves, and bringing

---

[246] Cook, Benjamin, 'The DWM Interview', DWM #500, p62.
[247] *The Unquiet Dead* (2005).
[248] *Planet of the Daleks* (1973).

to their knees those who set themselves up as gods. The novelty of *The God Complex* is that he is finally forced to direct such an attack against himself. He has to accept his fallibility as a hero.

His mistakes are not limited to misreading a situation and inadvertently putting others in danger, even if it is the trigger for his introspection in *The God Complex*. He also misreads others around him, even those closest to him. His assessment of the heroism and villainy of others is not always on the mark. In *The God Complex*, he is surprised by Rory's loss of faith in him, despite the harrowing events of the preceding story. He assumes that the projection of the Weeping Angels represents Amy's fear, unable to consider the possibility that his own failures might be what keeps her awake at night. The dialogue serves to highlight his lack of comprehension:

DOCTOR

Amy, they're not real.

AMY

What?

DOCTOR

They should have got us by now. Amy, look at me. Focus on me. It's your bad dream, that's all.

RORY

I don't even think they're for us.

Since 2005, almost every companion or near-companion of the Doctor is either underestimated or overly trusted. Mickey is cruelly put down by the ninth Doctor, and yet he becomes a hero despite the Doctor. Danny Pink is another example of a character whose heroism is discouraged because of the Doctor's own inadequacies and hang-ups (in this case his ambivalence towards the military). Either side of *The God Complex*, the Doctor can get it spectacularly wrong in his judgement of others, but after Rita and the Minotaur's challenge, he has at least begun to reflect on those kneejerk reactions, acknowledging and learning from his mistakes.

Danny Pink's example teaches him that love is not an emotion but a promise. Clara literally becomes his carer, when she visits the scared and vulnerable child on Gallifrey and teaches him about how fear can be his superpower[249]. His companions are no longer there just for assistance, or even to keep his excesses in check, they now serve to aid him in his hero's journey towards enlightenment.

The God Complex should have been a game changer in the Doctor's journey, but Whithouse holds back from fully reflecting the brutality of the plot in his script. The Doctor's self-directed anger is not as forceful or shocking as it could have been. His relationship with Amy and Rory is not soured as much as it could have been. The air of finality, of separation and resignation is compromised by the hint that the Doctor has not quite given up on himself or his companions. It takes another half a series to finally break the Doctor, but without doubt, the events of *The God Complex* were instrumental in putting into motion this shift in the Doctor's self-understanding.

---

[249] *Listen.*

THE CHANGING ROLE OF THE COMPANION

Although the Doctor is dramatically redefined as a hero who is in need of redemption, the most enduring legacy of *The God Complex* is that it offers a story based explanation for the changing role of his companions under Steven Moffat. The Doctor finds his redemption, but his relationship with his chosen followers has never quite been the same. In a far more radical reworking of their role than that which Russell T Davies introduced with *Rose* (2005), from this point on, companions are no longer full-time time-travellers. In one sense this is the natural extension of 2005's focus on the companion's world outside of her involvement with the Doctor, but crucially, journeying in the TARDIS ceases to be an escape.

Rose and Donna trade their disappointing, under-achieving lives for the trip of a lifetime, not in order to show that they have no value back home, but because their untapped potential is released in countless adventures with the Time Lord. They are therefore depicted as special because of who they are, not for what they have achieved. But Martha is different: ambitious and good at what she does, she is already carving out a career when she first encounters the Doctor. She makes the ultimate sacrifice, casting her vocation aside in order to follow him.

The fact that Martha is portrayed as the spurned lover seems a somewhat unenlightened perspective. Like Sarah Jane before her, her expertise becomes increasingly irrelevant and rarely tapped. Her most heroic moment comes in *Last of the Time Lords*, when in blind faith she takes on the role of the Doctor's evangelist, inspiring others to worship him as the saviour of the universe. But by this point she could be anyone, even a temp from Chiswick. Martha has come to accept a one-way, unconditional love at the expense of her desires and needs, giving in to an unequal relationship.

Martha's ultimate fate reveals a less satisfactory conclusion. Even Russell T Davies failed to completely break away from the enduring legacy of the traditional role of the companion. Whilst it is true that after she leaves the Doctor her career is back on track, she is subsequently seen working for both UNIT and Torchwood[250], without any moral scruples about how these organisations might conflict with the Hippocratic Oath. Martha's journey is almost entirely undone when inexplicably she ends up with Rose's ex, Mickey, seemingly now working as freelance alien fighters[251]. The military side has now replaced the medical. The fact that Mickey is a familiar character to the viewers slightly obscures how the ending for Martha is not really all that different from Leela's or Jo Grant's[252].

Under Russell T Davies, the companion is totally defined by their relationship with the Doctor, sacrificing, loving, protecting and defending him. Giving the viewers a window into their backgrounds serves merely to highlight their commitment to the Doctor, providing points of tension and jealousy for those left on the

---

[250] *The Sontaran Stratagem / The Poison Sky, The Stolen Earth / Journey's End*, and the **Torchwood** episodes *Reset, Dead Man Walking* and *A Day in the Death* (all 2008).
[251] *The End of Time* part 2.
[252] In *The Invasion of Time* (1978) and *The Green Death* respectively.

sidelines. But crucially, none of it is for his benefit. He might need the company, or need that small voice of conscience to rein in his excesses, but with the possible exception of Wilf Mott, none of Russell T Davies' characters go so far as to think their hero needs saving. They see themselves as the ones being saved, whether from a rundown estate (Rose), a dead-end job (Donna) or, ironically, a career-distracting infatuation (Martha).

Amy marks the turning point as 'the girl who waited'[253]. The Raggedy Man is a curse not a blessing, harming her development as a child because he let her down. It couldn't be more different from the 10th Doctor's faithfulness to Reinette[254]. In Room 7, Amy's greatest fear is being let down, seeing her seven-year-old self, sat on a suitcase, waiting for the Doctor to return as he promised. Yet the Doctor assumes that to escape the prison, he needs to destroy her faith in him. He also assumes that Amy is the reason why they have been brought there in the first place. Both are of course a symptom of his god complex, and with him successfully breaking the Minotaur's curse, his reasoning seems on the mark. The Rubik's cube is only solved at the point in which the Doctor realises that the Minotaur feeds off faith and not fear, and so the image deliberately signals to the viewer that after his earlier mistake, the Doctor has finally got it right. But another tantalising possibility is worth considering here. What if the Doctor has got it wrong again and our implicit faith in him has led us to make a similarly false conclusion? What if it was his faith in himself that was the primary

---

[253] *The Eleventh Hour.*
[254] *The Girl in the Fireplace* (2006).

target all along, and not Amy's? After all, there was a room for him too[255].

Is it really just a coincidence that the 'Do Not Disturb' sign falls precisely at this point? Every time a person is consumed by the Minotaur, an object falls to the floor – pages from Lucy's notebook, Joe's dice and cuffs, Howie's glasses and the telephone Rita was holding. And now as the Minotaur dies, it is the 'Do Not Disturb' sign. This is the death of the lonely god, the Doctor himself, mirrored in the Minotaur. All the others die because of their faith, but the Doctor is dying because he is being stripped of his.

Amy still believes in the Doctor to an extent. She needs to go through this change of faith, from blind hope to questioning provisionality, but the process started long before *The God Complex*. The issue is how far Amy is prepared to acknowledge her doubts. We have a hint earlier in the episode that her faith might not be as resolute as her actions and words appear to suggest. When Rory suggests to her that Rita might be in danger as they watch the Doctor befriending her, he flinches, explaining; 'Ooh. Sorry. The last time I said something like that, you hit me with your shoe. And you literally had to sit down and unlace it first.' Instead of hitting Rory for doubting the Doctor, Amy smiles affectionately. The object of Amy's desire, her true hero, is Rory not the Doctor, a fact brought out in *Amy's Choice*, and *A Good Man Goes To War* (2011) to name but two. Losing faith in himself, the Doctor is finally accepting that his companions are no worse off without him. Their

---

[255] It is also worth noting that the ventriloquists' dummies follow the Doctor's movements, keeping their eyes and heads turned towards him, even when there are others in the room.

lives have meaning, adventure and fulfilment, despite him rather than because of him. The Minotaur can only die when the Doctor figuratively dies to himself.

Since the Doctor is made aware that the attitudes of his admirers have, or need to be, changed, he can no longer justify whisking people away from their regular lives on a full-time, all or nothing basis. It is time they found the extraordinary in the ordinary (like the Ood on the lavatory). He should not be giving them any reason to hope or even want for him to come back again. Every adventure must feel like the last. This is what he intended for Martha after Rose, but for both of them, just that one adventure was impossible. By trying to set up a home for Amy and Rory at the end of *The God Complex*, he proves to himself that he is finally ready to redefine the boundaries. The Doctor is getting there, but the fact that the front door is TARDIS blue is a sure sign that his redemption and sacrifice are not quite complete.

This shift in power means that the Doctor can no longer expect his friends to always choose him over other competing interests. It's not a situation he feels entirely comfortable with and he still resorts to the occasional coercive measure in order to command their attention[256]. But by and large he has accepted that this is the way it has to be. Amy, Rory and Clara are now able to hold down regular jobs (modelling/writing, nursing and teaching) and still travel with the Doctor. Theoretically, he could have kept them on board full time, waiting for them to grow tired of the itinerant lifestyle before returning them to the point at which he first met

---

[256] *Into the Dalek* (2014).

them (as he tried to with Martha), but that would not alter the dynamic, and the Doctor's god complex would be reinforced. Travelling with the Doctor is not a sabbatical from life's daily chores, but part of them. Amy reasons that he is leaving them on Earth to save them, but in reality he is saving himself too. They will still be put in danger. The adventures will continue, but it is no longer all about him, or even primarily about him.

In the next episode, *Closing Time*, the 11th Doctor experiments with the idea of dispensing with the old 'all of time and space' trick. By knocking on Craig Owens' door, instead of materialising the TARDIS inside, he is clearly trying to interact with friends by using the normal rules of engagement (he does the same with Amy and Rory[257], and Clara[258]). Whilst his companions can be part-time, he remains ambivalent towards his own status as the eternal wanderer. For him, the TARDIS is not just a means of transport, it is home. He tries to mimic the newfound freedom of his friends, by taking on various temporary positions (shop worker, caretaker), but it can never be a permanent solution. Clara may be able to master being the Doctor[259], but he can never successfully step into her shoes.

Amy's faith in the Doctor is not completely destroyed. Even Rory has still not completely closed the door on future travels. So when, in Amy's word, the Doctor later 'comes to stay' in an effort to interact with his friends in their world instead of taking them away, Rory's dad makes a telling point as the Doctor tries to leave:

---

257 *Pond Life.*
258 *The Bells of Saint John* (2013), *Time of the Doctor.*
259 *Flatline, Death in Heaven.*

DOCTOR

Dear me. I'd better get going. Things to do, worlds to save, swings to swing on. Look, I know, you both have lives here. Beautiful, messy lives. That is what makes you so fabulously human. You don't want to give them up. I understand.

BRIAN

Actually, it's you they can't give up, Doctor. And I don't think they should. Go with him. Go save every world you can find. Who else has that chance? Life will still be here.[260]

Amy's faith has matured. She no longer sees the Doctor as the infallible superhero who, if stripped of his powers and essential goodness, would be useless[261]. It doesn't matter that he gets it wrong, or that sometimes there are no winners. But he is still worth following, because without hope life is not the romantic ideal the Doctor, as an envious outsider, imagines it to be. Is it not being able to give up an addiction, like continuing to smoke when fully aware of the health risks, or is it, as Brian thinks, a commitment to save worlds? Brian still sees the Doctor as a saviour figure, but for Rory and Amy, the hero can no longer be relied upon. In a reversal of the tension between those left behind and those called to follow, Brian actively encourages them to go. His intervention is needed to set them on their way again. Questioning faith perseveres despite the inadequacies of its object. It is a commitment more than an addiction.

---

[260] *The Power of Three* (2012).
[261] See especially her reaction in *Amy's Choice* to the Doctor being unable to bring Rory back to life.

The rebalancing of power under Steven Moffat extends to the narrative arcs, with Amy, River and Clara's stories all taking centre stage, reducing the Doctor to a bemused onlooker or confused detective. The downside of such a heightened role is the loss of a figure the audience can relate to. This leads to a greater need for other supporting characters such as Rita, Osgood, Perkins, Rigsy[262] and Shona[263] (all of them seen as 'almost' companions). Both Rory and Danny Pink are unable to fulfil such a role, with their own stories also being fantastical and shrouded in mystery for much of their run.

Russell T Davies highlighted the ordinariness of the companions, whilst Moffat took them into the realm of fantasy, making them as mysterious as the Doctor himself. The pendulum will no doubt swing back again, but with the Doctor at his most vulnerable, wary of developing attachments, both Amy and Clara attract him because they are puzzles to solve, not because of their human qualities or because they display a wide-eyed fascination with him.

The finality of Amy and Rory's departure in *The Angels Take Manhattan* (2012) presented a problem for Steven Moffat. How could he introduce the next companion without undermining the significance of the Doctor's changing understanding from *The God Complex* on? To emphasise the fact that he is no longer manipulating others into travelling with him, his relationship with Clara is revealed, eventually, to have been set up by Missy. It is a perfectly timed intervention: for the first time in his lives, the

---

[262] *Flatline, Face the Raven* (2015).
[263] *Last Christmas.*

Doctor is of a mindset neither to feel sorry for another unfulfilled human, nor to find a follower who will polish his ego. Instead he has a mystery to solve in Clara. It is an enigma he would have run away from had she displayed the traits of a typical companion. It is only because she is a woman who is not easily impressed, one who remains wary of his motivations, that he accepts the challenge.

With the ongoing story of the Doctor's quest to free himself from his god complex finally completed in *Death in Heaven*[264], the way has been paved for a more equitable partnership to come with future companions. He is ready to welcome others, to learn from and to teach, to be proven wrong and proven right, to be the best and the worst with. The journey from 'It's all about the Doctor' to 'It's all about the companion' is complete. Now it is time for a relationship of equals, of the kind we almost get with River Song and the Doctor, and with Clara and Me in series nine (2015).

Nearly Companions and Super-Fans

We have already seen how the 21st-century series regularly introduces 'nearly companions' who clearly represent an element of fandom. Such characters are more prone to hero-worship than the regular TARDIS travellers. For example, notice how Osgood's reaction to being confronted by a Zygon, is to pray to the Doctor to save her, even though she knows he is not in close proximity[265]. The stereotyped fans within the **Doctor Who** universe almost always

---

[264] Though he remains susceptible to temptation and relapse, particularly when he feels responsible for a friend's death (*The Girl Who Died, Hell Bent* (both 2015)), he no longer assumes he has done the right thing after playing god.
[265] *The Day of the Doctor.*

have a conservative, absolute faith, at least to begin with. When the Doctor is at the height of his god complex, these starry-eyed followers, for whom the Doctor can do no wrong, and who define their whole existence around him, are what he wishes his closest companions to be.

Foreshadowing Rose's tragic fate in *Doomsday* (2006), Elton is the only super-fan who, after finally meeting his hero, is forced to reconsider his faith. Fearing for the future of Rose and Jackie, he quotes Stephen King's maxim that salvation and damnation are one and the same[266]. He extols the virtues of the ordinary over journeying with the Time Lord. The Doctor breaks the hero-worship by confessing that he failed to save Elton's mother, when he was a boy. And yet, unable to help himself, the Doctor still assumes the mantle of a saviour, bringing back Elton's girlfriend but only as a face, trapped in a paving slab. This bittersweet victory is a visual example of Stephen King's point, but Elton chooses to focus on the positive side. The Doctor has become his saviour, after all. Part of the Doctor's god-complex is the belief that he can work all things together for good, and find the silver lining to every cloud. *Love & Monsters* (2006) shows just how far he is prepared to go with that fix-it mentality, and that perhaps sometimes the better option is to let go and walk away.

When the fifth Doctor meets his 10th regeneration, he assumes he is a fan, and though he expresses dread at the possibility of coming face to face with an overenthusiastic hero-worshipper, the idea

---

[266] *Love & Monsters.*

that he commands such a sheep-like following clearly boosts his ego:

> 'Okay, you're my biggest fan. Look, it's perfectly understandable. I go zooming around space and time, saving planets, fighting monsters and being well, let's be honest, pretty sort of marvellous, so naturally now and then people notice me.'[267]

The 11th Doctor makes no secret of the fact that he likes to make a show of being the hero: 'I'm being extremely clever up here, and there's no one to stand around looking impressed! What's the point in having you all?'[268] A similar phrase is used by Amy when the Doctor is unable to save Rory: 'What's the point of you?'[269] Just as the superhero is pointless to the fan if they don't save the day, so the fan is pointless to the superhero if they are not there to witness and applaud his or her actions.

Fan and hero need to meet each other's expectations in order to keep the illusion alive. But the stereotyped fan, as characterised in the show, would make for the most irritating of companions, both for the Doctor and the viewer. They can only ever be almost companions. Absolute faith and subservience are sycophantic and dull. This stereotype represents the extremes of conservative faith, the kind that a person with a god complex feeds off. This need for the would-be-hero to have a band of followers, is the very thing that Rita perceives after just a few minutes in the Doctor's

---

[267] 'Time Crash' (2007).
[268] *The Impossible Astronaut.*
[269] *Amy's Choice.*

company. Not only does he believe he can save her, but despite knowing that he shouldn't, he cannot help but ask her to travel with him.

DOCTOR

I brought them here. They'd say it was their choice, but offer a child a suitcase full of sweets and they'll take it. Offer someone all of time and space and they'll take that, too. Which is why you shouldn't. Which is why grown-ups were invented.

RITA

All of time and space, eh?

DOCTOR

And when we get out of this, I'll show you too.

RITA

I don't know what you are talking about. But whatever it was, I have a feeling you just did it again.

There are countless examples to back up Rita's assessment. Perhaps the most striking is when Jackson Lake, adopting the persona of the Doctor, attempts to put Rosetta in her place: 'the Doctor's companion does what the Doctor says'[270]. Whilst the 10th Doctor in that same story agrees with Lake that the companions are always telling them off, and later identifies their role as that of asking all the questions, the belief that they will ultimately do what

---

[270] *The Next Doctor.*

they are told is symptomatic of his god complex. The Doctor simply assumes that Rita will accept the offer, not by choice but by compulsion.

The new dynamic, introduced after the Doctor faces up to himself in the mirror of the Minotaur, is that his companions must always have the choice[271]. Choice plays a vital role in *The God Complex*. The faith stolen by the Minotaur takes away freedom quite literally as the characters automatically chant 'Praise him.' Immediately after this exchange between Rita and the Doctor, she says for the first time, 'Praise him.' Even Rita has succumbed to a regressive, unreasoned, automatic faith. If, in keeping with the psychological interpretations of the Minotaur myth, the worship of the Minotaur is a cipher for the worship of the Doctor, then the faith of his near companions, idealised companions and actual companions, is parodied to the extreme. Of course, even his most submissive followers are not brainwashed, possessed or psychotic, but the point is that so long as the Doctor leads and manipulates them with his god complex, then they may as well be. If the Doctor did manage to save Rita, the implication is that she would have accepted the call and in so doing would have given up everything, including her religion and career, to follow him.

In a delicious and surely intentional irony, the sheep-like mentality of the hero-worshipper is of a kind with Gibbis' desire to be oppressed. In blind trust and obedience, the human idol or constructed god is invested with salvific power over all aspects of

---

[271] Clara calls the shots when he asks her to join him, telling him to come back the next day (*The Bells of Saint John*).

life. All control is given over to the object of faith. The idol is always there in the worshipper's head, watching over their every move. When the Doctor in the CCTV room assumes the Big Brother perspective, all seeing, all knowing, it is a metaphor for the way in which he gets into the head of his followers. The history books show how the cry of salvation and the acceptance of oppression often go hand in hand. In many ways, though the Doctor writes off his whole species as cowards, Gibbis is the logical extension of the kind of followers a person with a god complex creates. There is a symmetry between the Doctor's self-directed anger and his criticisms of Gibbis. The Doctor is driven to face up to the nightmare of himself and of his ideal followers. He is learning that a friend who can say no, and decide not to feed his ego, is better than a companion who might, like Gibbis, happily be enslaved. If Rita survived and if the Doctor could win while keeping his god complex intact, she would have become like Gibbis, a participator in an unequal relationship.

SO LONG – BUT WHAT ABOUT THE FISH?

One of the most puzzling features of *The God Complex* is the fishbowl. In an episode so tightly structured and full of well-signalled symbolism, the viewer is forced to question its meaning. Unlike almost every other incidental feature, there are no links to Whithouse's major influences, the Minotaur myth, *1984* or *The Shining*. A quick scan of **Doctor Who** canon also fails to explain its appearance.

In the midst of the Minotaur smashing up the spa, the Doctor asks Amy to move the fish, much to her surprise. Later, we see her place the fishbowl on a table, with the Doctor and Rita looking on. When they next appear, Gibbis proceeds to eat them.

In the first scene, Rory has just been knocked unconscious by the creature, but the Doctor seems more concerned about the fish.

DOCTOR

Pond, bring the fish.

AMY

What, the fish? Oh, the fish.

At the most basic level, this scene could be foreshadowing the moment when Gibbis eats the fish. The fish would therefore serve no other purpose than to provide a visual reason to dislike Gibbis. But if this was the case, it would have made more sense to position the fish in the reception in the first place, introducing them early, in one of the many establishing shots of the episode. The most common interpretation is to see the fish as an example of the Doctor's failure to be the saviour, or even more pointedly, of his direct involvement in the fate of others (after all, if he hadn't asked Amy to move them, Gibbis might never have seen them). This interpretation works quite well, given that the Doctor explicitly says to Rita that he brought Amy and Rory to the prison. The correspondence breaks down however, because the Doctor reassesses the situation, believing Amy to be the reason why the trio have been brought to the ship.

To fully appreciate the symbolism of the fish, we have to consider the immediate context as well as Amy's role in the scene. Despite her husband having been knocked unconscious, Amy blindly follows the Doctor's instruction. Rory then regains consciousness to find Rita and not Amy showing concern for his welfare. Instead Amy is focused on finding the Doctor. With typical Pinter-like economy, Whithouse emphasises the contrast using some quickfire dialogue.

RORY

Somebody hit me. Was it Amy?

RITA

Rory, are you all right?

AMY

We should find the Doctor.

The Doctor is in his 'the companion does what the Doctor tells him' mode, and Amy, though slightly thrown, simply obeys[272]. The fact

---

[272] A very sharp contrast to *The Eleventh Hour*, when Amy disobeys the Doctor and goes into the room containing Prisoner Zero, much to the Doctor's irritation; 'Stay away from that door! Do not touch

that the Doctor would even care about the fish over Rory is perhaps to emphasis his Messiah complex – the belief that he can save every living thing (including as we have seen, the Minotaur itself). It might also be a reminder that he is an alien and does not make human-based assessments of the relative worth of different creatures' lives. But what matters here, is Amy's obedience.

In the very next scene, when Amy goes looking for the Doctor, she finds instead her nightmare room. At this point the viewer is not shown the contents as Rita pulls her back and Amy brushes it aside, simply saying that it was weird. Later we discover that she has seen her younger self, waiting in vain for the Doctor. Reading back the scene with hindsight, in the midst of trying to find the Doctor, Amy has been reminded of that terrible fear of never seeing him again. Her unquestioning obedience, shown by the ridiculous decision to pick up the fishbowl despite Rory's fall, is not necessarily symptomatic of a belief that his eccentric ways might bring salvation. Obeying his instructions could be her way of keeping him. It is an action driven by a fear that one day he might no longer need her. She does what she is told, because it gives her a continued role. It gives the Doctor a reason to still want her.

The timing of Amy finding a new home for the goldfish bowl is also significant. Rory has just pointed out to the Doctor that not all victories are about saving the universe. Only by distancing himself

---

that door! Listen to me, do not open that. Why does no-one ever listen to me? Do I just have a face that nobody listens to?' Here he comes across as an exasperated parent. Even though Amy is dressed as a police officer and has him handcuffed to the radiator, the Doctor still believes he can command her obedience.

from the Doctor is Rory able to understand Howie, learning that his greatest victory was overcoming his stammer. After a shot of the laid-out bodies of Joe and Howie, the camera cuts to Amy still blindly carrying out the Doctor's instructions as she places the goldfish bowl on the table. Would she have had a greater victory if one of her counsellors had successfully resolved those issues that had been triggered by her encounter with the Raggedy Man?

The fact that Gibbis eats the poor fish is loaded with symbolism because of this earlier scene. In acting the hero, the Doctor ends up feeding the Tivolian. His failure to control the fate of the fish is neatly contrasted with his freedom of choice when it comes to eating the apple near the beginning of the episode[273]. Notice how the apples are inside an identical glass bowl. The viewer might think the Doctor detests the fruit[274], but he is freely able to defy our expectations. When it comes to the fish it is the Doctor's expectations that are confounded.

---

[273] The link between the apple and choice goes back to the Garden of Eden mythology, and is commonly associated with temptation. In the Judgement of Paris myth for example, Paris is tasked by Zeus with deciding which of three goddesses should receive a golden apple, intended for 'the most beautiful one.' They attempt to buy the apple by offering him respectively power, wealth and love. He picks the latter, abducting Helen of Troy, causing the start of the Trojan War (interestingly, Theseus too, long after defeating the Minotaur, would go on to abduct Helen). The temptation that the Doctor succumbs to in *The God Complex*, is as ever, the Time Lord 'sin' of intervention, and the impact can be just as devastating and far reaching.

[274] *The Eleventh Hour.*

By moving the fish, Amy has become an accessory, not to the Doctor saving the universe again, but to the Doctor keeping alive (through the symbol of food) a character who represents the antithesis of what his heroism is all about. Gibbis does not need or want a saviour, and he undergoes no change of heart after meeting the Doctor. He is not liberated, only set free from one manipulative system, ready to be enslaved again by another. More disturbingly, the Doctor is not working alone. Not only does his god complex blind his followers to his mistakes, it pulls them in as participants.

The story of the fish, far from being light relief, emphasises the futility of the Doctor's faith in himself, and the unreasonableness behind his expectation of success and his demands upon his friends. It also highlights the negative impact his god complex has upon his followers, twisting their priorities and turning them into unquestioning lackeys. As much as the Doctor likes to value freedom from oppression, his interventions can be counterproductive. His companions are always at their most effective when they are prepared to question and challenge the Doctor. To allow them that power, he has to let them go. He must accept that it has to be their choice whether to join him or reject his advances. He can only succeed by adjusting his self-image, stripping himself of his god complex.

Yet again, timing is everything. This time, just before Gibbis is drawn to the fish, the Doctor has come face to face with Room 11, putting the 'Do Not Disturb' sign over the door. Just as the nightmares have been leaking out of the rooms literally, so too the symbolism of what that room might contain leaks out into the scene with Gibbis and the fish. I have argued that the Doctor's fear is the death of his most faithful companion, the TARDIS. Such a loss would trigger all sorts of associations: the fear of losing his powers, of having to settle down, of having nothing to lure companions with, of inadvertently causing the cracks in the universe whilst trying to save it. But the TARDIS is also the Doctor's conscience at times. She makes up for his bad choices by giving him the opportunity to make amends, by being choosy about who to let in and by deciding where to land[275]. Losing her would be the ultimate failure. The Doctor might be able to deny his human companions choice, but it doesn't work with the TARDIS.

The Doctor's response to fear is to keep the skeletons in the cupboard, and carry on regardless. But outside, his fears are being realised. Gibbis is about to eat the fish that the Doctor assumed he could save; the fish he instructed Amy to move. If his friends realise they are no longer helping him to save the universe, then what possible reason could they have to follow him? If he isn't the hero his god complex tells him he is, then does that make him a tyrant instead, helping or even creating Gibbis-like followers, who are quite happy to be fed and enslaved? The nightmare scenario for someone with a god complex, is that he ends up, like the liberated owners of the ship, creating greater injustices than the ones he'd tried to free others from.

---

[275] *The Doctor's Wife.*

BIBLIOGRAPHY

Books

Arnold, Jon, *Rose*. **The Black Archive #1**. Edinburgh, Obverse Books 2016. ISBN 9781909031371.

Barr, Jason and Camille Mustachio, (eds), *The Language Of Doctor Who from Shakespeare to Alien Tongues*. New York, Rowman & Littlefield Publishers, 2014. ISBN 9781442234802.

Bazzell, Pascal D, *Urban Ecclesiology: Gospel of Mark, Familia Dei and a Filipino Community Facing Homelessness*. Edinburgh, T & T Clark, 2015. ISBN 9780567659804.

The Bible, New International Version. Hodder & Stoughton, 2011. ISBN 9781444701509.

Borges, Jorge Luis, *Labyrinths: Selected Stories and Other Writings*. Donald Yates and James E Irby, eds, London, Penguin, 2000. ISBN 9780141184845.

Bourke, Joanna, *Fear: A Cultural History*. London, Virago Press, 2005. ISBN 9781844081561.

Brummer, Vincent, *The Model Of Love*. Cambridge, Cambridge University Press, 1993. ISBN 9780521444637.

Campbell, Joseph, *The Hero with a Thousand Faces*. 1949. New Jersey, Bollingden, 2004. ISBN 9780691119243.

Chapman, James, *Inside the TARDIS: The Worlds of Doctor Who – A Cultural History*. London, IB Tauris 2006. ISBN 9781845111632.

Crome, Andrew, and James Mcgrath, eds, *Time and Relative Dimensions in Faith*. London, Dartman, Longman and Todd, 2013. ISBN 9780232530216.

Danielewski, Mark Z, *House of Leaves*. New York, Pantheon Books, 2000. ISBN 9780385603102.

Dante Alighieri, *Inferno*. 1320. London, Penguin Classics, 2006. ISBN 9780140448955.

Davies, Russell T, and Benjamin Cook, *The Writer's Tale: The Final Chapter*. London, BBC Books, 2010. ISBN 9781846078613.

Dawkins, Richard, *The God Delusion*. London, Black Swan, 2007. ISBN 9780552773317.

Decker, Kevin, *Who is Who? The Philosophy of Doctor Who*. Tauris, 2013. ISBN 9781780765532.

Dürrenmatt, Friedrich, *Selected Writings: Fictions* vol 2. University of Chicago Press, 2006. ISBN 9780226174297.

Fingeroth, Danny, *Superman on the Couch*. Continuum, 2004. ISBN 9780826415400.

Fowler, James, *Stages of Faith: The Psychology of Human Development and the Quest for Meaning*. San Francisco, Harper and Row, 1981. ISBN 9780060628666.

Garner, Ross, Melissa Beattie and Una McCormack, eds, *Impossible Worlds, Impossible Things*. Cambridge Scholars Publishing, 2010. ISBN 9781443819602.

Gillat, Gary, *Doctor Who from A to Z*. London, BBC Books, 1998. ISBN 9780563405894.

Gray, Jeffrey Alan, *The Psychology of Fear and Stress*. London, Weidenfeld and Nicolson, London, 1971. ISBN 9780303760559.

Hulke, Malcolm and Terrance Dicks, *The Making of Doctor Who*. Piccolo Books, 1972. ISBN 9780330232036.

Jung, CG, *The Collected Works of CG Jung*, fourth edition. Sir Herbert Read, ed, New Jersey, Princeton University Press, 1975.

Jung, Carl, *Essays on a Science of Mythology: The Myth of the Divine Child and the Mysteries of Eleusis*. Princeton, Princeton University Press, 1949.

Kaveney, Roz, *Superheroes! Capes and Crusaders in Comics and Films*. London, IB Tauris, 2007. ISBN 9781845115692.

King, Stephen, *The Shining*. New York, Doubleday, 1977. ISBN 9780385121675.

Layton, David, *The Humanism of Doctor Who*. Jefferson, McFarland & Company, 2012. ISBN 9780786466733.

Lewis, Courtland, and Paula Smithka, eds, *Doctor Who and Philosophy*. Chicago, Open Court Publishing Company, 2010. ISBN 9780812696882.

McKee, Gabriel, *The Gospel According to Science Fiction*. Louisville, Westminster John Knox Press, 2007. ISBN 9780664229016.

Orwell, George, *Nineteen Eighty-Four*. 1949. London, Penguin Classics, 2013. ISBN 9780141393049.

Pausanias, *Description of Greece*, Books 1-2. Second century BCE. Cambridge, MA, Loeb, 1989. ISBN 9780674991040.

Pramaggiore, Maria, and Tom Wallis, *Film: A Critical Introduction*. London, Laurence King Publishing, 2005. ISBN 9781856694421.

Rumens, Carol, *De Chirico's Threads*. Seren, 2010. ISBN 9781854115348.

Saunders, Ben, *Do the Gods Wear Capes?* London, Continuum, 2011. ISBN 9780826441980.

Shakespeare, William, *A Midsummer Night's Dream*. 1600. Ware, Wordsworth Classics, 1992. ISBN 9781853260308.

Shermer, Michael, *The Believing Brain*. London, Robinson, 2011. ISBN 9781780335292.

Sleight, Graham, *The Doctor's Monsters*. London, Tauris, 2012. ISBN 9781848851788.

Szirtes, George, *Reel*. 2005. Bloodaxe Books, 2014. ISBN 9781852246761.

Periodicals

Doctor Who Magazine (DWM). Marvel UK, Panini, BBC 1979-.

Arnopp, Jason, 'Ghost Writer'. DWM #492, cover date December 2015.

Bignell, Richard, 'An Unearthly Beginning'. DWM #467, cover date November 2013.

Cook, Benjamin, 'The Nightmare Man'. DWM #432, cover date April 2011.

Cook, Benjamin, 'The God Complex'. DWM #438, cover date September 2011.

Cook, Benjamin, 'Favourite Worst Nightmare'. DWM #439, cover date October 2011.

Cook, Benjamin, 'The DWM Interview'. DWM #500, cover date July 2016.

Kibble-White, Graham, 'The God Complex'. DWM #440, cover date November 2011.

Pixley, Andrew, 'The God Complex'. *The Doctor Who Companion* vol 5: *The Eleventh Doctor*. DWM Special Edition #31, cover date August 2012.

Kibble-White, Graham, 'Parasites and Predators'. *The Essential Doctor Who* #5: *Monsters*, cover date June 2015.

Radio Times. BBC Magazines, Immediate Media Company 1921-.

Doctor Who Tenth Anniversary Special, November 1973.

Sandmel, Samuel, 'Parallelomania'. *Journal Of Biblical Literature* 81, 1962.

Tilney, Martin, 'Waiting for Redemption in the House of Asterion: A Stylistic Analysis'. *Open Journal of Modern Linguistics*, vol 2 no 2, 2012, pp51-56.

Walters, Glen, 'Understanding the Popular Appeal of Horror Cinema: An Integrated-Interactive Model'. *Journal of Media Psychology*, vol 9 no 2, Spring, 2004

Zillman, Dolf, 'Excitation Transfer in Communication-Mediated Aggressive Behaviour'. *Journal of Experimental Social Psychology*, 7.4, 1971.

Television

The Apprentice. BBC, 2005-.

Battlestar Galactica. Glen A Larson Productions, David Eick Productions, R&D TV, Universal Television, 1978-80, 2003-2009.

Being Human. Touchpaper Television, 2008-2013.

Blake's 7. BBC, 1978-1981.

Buffy the Vampire Slayer. Mutant Enemy Productions, 20th Century Fox Television, 1997-2003.

Doctor Who. BBC, 1963-.

Firefly. Mutant Enemy Productions, 20th Century Fox Television, 2002.

The Kumars at No. 42. Hatrick Productions, 2001-2006.

No Angels. World Productions, 2004-2006.

The Sarah Jane Adventures. BBC Wales, 2007-2011.

The Day of the Clown, 2008.

The Nightmare Man, 2010.

Death of the Doctor, 2010.

Sherlock. Hartswood Films, BBC Wales, WGBH, 2010-.

Torchwood. BBC Wales, BBC Worldwide Canadian Broadcasting Corporation, Starz Entertainment, 2006-11.

Greeks Bearing Gifts, 2006.

Film

Ascher, Rodney, dir, *Room 237*, 2012.

Ball, Wes, dir, *The Maze Runner*, Gotham Group, Temple Hill Entertainment, TSG Entertainment, 2014.

Becker, Josh, dir, *Hercules in the Maze of the Minotaur*, 1994.

Burton, Tim, dir, *Charlie and the Chocolate Factory*, Warner Bros, 2005.

Columbus, Chris, dir, *Percy Jackson and the Olympians: The Lightening Thief*, 1492 Pictures, 2010.

Craven, Wes, dir, *Scream*, Dimension Films, 1996.

Flanagan, Mike, dir, *Hush*, Intrepid Pictures, 2016.

Friedkin, dir, *The Exorcist*, Hoya Productions, 1973.

Hitchcock, Alfred, dir, *Pyscho,* Paramount Pictures, 1960.

Holland, Tom, dir, *Child's Play*, United Artists, 1988.

Hooper, Tobe, dir, Poltergeist, MGM, Amblin Entertainment, 1982.

Kubrick, Stanley, dir, *The Shining*, The Producer Circle Company, Peregrine Productions, Hawk Films, 1980.

Lucas, George, dir, *Star Wars IV: A New Hope*, Lucasfilm Ltd, 1977.

Natali, Vincenzo, dir, *Cube*, Trimark Pictures, 1997.

Spielberg, Steven, dir, *Jaws*, Zanuck/Brown Productions, 1975.

Wallace, Tommy Lee, dir, *It,* Lorrimer Productions, 1990.

Wan, James, dir, *Dead Silence*, Universal Pictures, 2007.

Zwicky, Karl, dir, *Sinbad and the Minotaur*, 2011.

Stage Plays

Harsent, David, and Harrison Birtwhistle, *The Minotaur: A Libretto*. 2008.

Whithouse, Toby, *Jump Mr Maniloff, Jump*. 2010.

Music

The Police, 'Every Breath You Take'. A&M Records, 1983.

Radio

Adams, Douglas, **The Hitchhiker's Guide to the Galaxy**, BBC Radio 4. 1978-80.

Gaming

Destiny of the Doctors. Studio Fish, BBC Multimedia, 1997.

Half-Life 2. Valve Corporation, Sierra Entertainment, 2004.

Monkey Island. LucasArts, 1990-2009.

Visual Art

Michelangelo, 'The Last Judgement'. 1536-41.

Picasso, Pablo, 'Minotauromachy'. 1935.

Rubens, Peter Paul, 'The Fall of Icarus'. 1636.

Titian, 'Bacchus and Ariadne'. 1522-23.

Web

'An Interview with Toby Whithouse'. BBC **Doctor Who** website, 10 September 2011.

http://www.bbc.co.uk/mobile/tv/doctorwho/news/news_1009201
1_01/index.shtml. Accessed 13 August 2016.

'The Fourth Dimension'. BBC **Doctor Who** website.
http://www.bbc.co.uk/programmes/articles/5P6l2V5qtX99tycT3qZ
SlDC/the-fourth-dimension. Accessed 13 August 2016.

Gallifrey Base. http://gallifreybase.com/forum/. Accessed 16
August 2016.

'Is CCTV Creeping too Far?'. BBC News, 20 January 2011.
http://www.bbc.co.uk/news/magazine-12224075. Accessed 13
August 2016.

'Script Doctors'. What Noise Productions, 24 November 2005.
http://www.whatnoise.co.uk/DEEJSAINT/WORDS/Entries/2005/11/
24_TOBY_WHITHOUSE_2005.html. Accessed 16 August 2016.

'The Psychology of Scary Movies'. Filmmaker IQ.
http://filmmakeriq.com/lessons/the-psychology-of-scary-movies.
Accessed 13 August 2016.

'Toby Whithouse: BBC Writersroom Interviews **Being Human**
Writer and Creator, Toby Whithouse'. BBC Writers Room, 2012.
http://www.bbc.co.uk/writersroom/writers-lab/be-inspired/toby-
whithouse. Accessed 13 August 2016.

'Adaddinsane', 'Toby Whithouse Q & A: A Report'. 4 March 2009.
http://adaddinsane.blogspot.co.uk/2009/03/toby-whithouse-q-
report.html. Accessed 13 August 2016.

Alexander, Ruth, 'Are There Really 100,000 New Christian Martyrs
Every Year?'. *BBC Magazine*, 12 November 2013.

http://www.bbc.co.uk/news/magazine-24864587. Accessed 13 August 2016.

Ashir-Perrin, Emily, '**Doctor Who** 4/12 NYC Premiere Screening Q & A Transcript!'. Tor, 12 April 2011. http://www.tor.com/2011/04/12/doctor-who-412-nyc-premiere-screening-qaa-transcript/. Accessed 13 August 2016.

Byrne, Joseph, 'Mise-En-Scene in Stanley Kubrick's *The Shining*'. ENGL245 Film Form and Culture, University of Maryland, Fall 2013. https://engl245umd.wordpress.com/2013/09/27/mise-en-scene-in-stanley-kubricks-the-shining/. Accessed 13 August 2016.

Carlisle, Clare, 'Is Religion Based On Fear?'. *The Guardian*, 2 December 2013. http://www.theguardian.com/commentisfree/belief/2013/dec/02/bertrand-russell-philosopher-religion-fear-christian. Accessed 13 August 2016.

Ciment, Michel, 'Kubrick on *The Shining*: An Interview with Michel Ciment'. The Kubrick Site. http://www.visual-memory.co.uk/amk/doc/interview.ts.html. Accessed 13 August 2016.

Crome, Andrew, 'Time Travel Through Faith'. BBC Religion and Ethics, 22 November 2013. http://www.bbc.co.uk/religion/0/24924746. Accessed 16 August 2016.

Diamond, Stephen, 'Why Myths Still Matter (Part Four): Facing Your Inner Minotaur and Following Your Ariadnean Thread'. *Psychology Today*, 18 December 2009. https://www.psychologytoday.com/blog/evil-deeds/200912/why-myths-still-matter-part-four-facing-your-inner-minotaur-and-following. Accessed 13 August 2016.

Dominiguez-Cheo, Amanda, '**Doctor Who**: A Hero's Journey'. *The Artifice*, 3 July 2014. http://the-artifice.com/doctor-who-hero-journey. Accessed 13 August 2016.

Dowden, Craig, 'Why You Should Believe in Luck'. *Psychology Today*, 9 June 2014. https://www.psychologytoday.com/blog/the-leaders-code/201406/why-you-should-believe-in-luck. Accessed 13 August 2016.

Drayna, Dennis, 'First Genes Found for Stammering'. *The British Stammering Association*, 1 June 2010. http://www.stammering.org/speaking-out/articles/first-genes-found-stammering. Accessed 13 August 2016.

Frick, Alice, and Donald Bull, 'Science Fiction: BBC Report'. 1962. BBC Archive. http://www.bbc.co.uk/archive/doctorwho/6400.shtml. Accessed 13 August 2016.

Fuller, Gavin, '**Doctor Who** *The God Complex*: BBC One Review'. *The Telegraph*, 17 September 2011 http://www.telegraph.co.uk/culture/tvandradio/doctor-who/8768248/Doctor-Who-The-God-Complex-BBC-One-review.html. Accessed 13 August 2016.

Gander, Kashmira, 'Halloween and Horror Films: Why do we Enjoy Being Scared?'. *The Independent*, 29 October 2015. http://www.independent.co.uk/life-style/health-and-families/features/halloween-horror-films-movies-scared-a6713446.html. Accessed 13 August 2016.

Garcia, Brittany, 'Minotaur'. *Ancient History Encyclopaedia*, 1 September 2013. http://www.ancient.eu/Minotaur/. Accessed 13 August 2016.

Glieberman, Owen, 'Room 237'. *Entertainment Weekly*, 1 April 2013. http://www.ew.com/article/2013/04/01/room-237. Accessed 13 August 2016.

Goldhill, Olivia, 'Why Are We So Scared of Clowns?'. *The Telegraph*, 7 December 2015. Accessed 13 August 2016. http://www.telegraph.co.uk/culture/halloween/11194653/Why-are-we-so-scared-of-clowns.html. Accessed 13 August 2016.

Hewett, Ivan, 'The Minotaur: Father and Son Venture into the Labyrinth'. *The Telegraph*, 10 April 2008. http://www.telegraph.co.uk/culture/theatre/3672454/The-Minotaur-father-and-son-venture-into-the-labyrinth.html. Accessed 13 August 2016.

Jameson, Richard, 'Kubrick's *Shining*'. 1980. FilmComment. http://www.filmcomment.com/article/stanley-kubrick-the-shining/. Accessed 13 August 2016.

Keogh, Garrett, 'Toby Whithouse Answers Your Questions: Part 3'. BBC, 10 February 2011. http://www.bbc.co.uk/blogs/beinghuman/2011/02/toby_whithouse_answers_your_qu_2.html. Accessed 13 August 2016.

Lankford, Adam, 'Martyr Myth: Inside the Minds of Suicide Bombers'. *New Scientist*, 3 July 2013. https://www.newscientist.com/article/mg21929240-200-martyr-myth-inside-the-minds-of-suicide-bombers/. Accessed 13 August 2016.

Lane, Megan, 'Why Do We Believe in Luck?'. *BBC Magazine*, 6 April 2011. http://www.bbc.co.uk/news/magazine-12934253. Accessed 13 August 2016.

Leith, Sam, 'Do You Know What Today's Kids Need? Thumb Amputation, That's What'. *The Guardian*, 2 November 2009. http://www.theguardian.com/books/2009/nov/01/sam-leith-childrens-films-books. Accessed 13 August 2016.

Martin, William, '10 Things We Learned From **Doctor Who** Writer Toby Whithouse's Twitter Q & A'. *Cultbox*, 1 May 2015. http://www.cultbox.co.uk/features/trivia/10-things-we-learned-from-doctor-who-writer-toby-whithouses-twitter-qa. Accessed 13 August 2016.

McGonigal, Kelly, 'How to Make Stress Your Friend'. TED Talk, 4 September 2013. https://www.youtube.com/watch?v=RcGyVTAoXEU. Accessed 13 August 2016.

McGreal, Chris, 'September 11 Conspiracy Theories Continue to Abound.' *The Guardian*, 5 September 2011. https://www.theguardian.com/world/2011/sep/05/september-11-conspiracy-theories. Accessed 13 August 2016.

Melina, Remy, 'Impulsive Gamblers are More Suspicious, Study Suggests'. Live Science, 29 June 2011. http://www.livescience.com/14839-impulsive-gamblers-superstitious.html. Accessed 13 August 2016.

Moffat, Steven and Peter Capaldi, 'The Doctor: A Different Kind of Hero'. BBC, 14 September 2015.

http://www.bbc.co.uk/programmes/p032j2qp. Accessed 13 August 2016.

Nededog, Jethro, 'Comic-Con 2011 Meets **Doctor Who**'s Matt Smith: 10 Behind-The-Scenes Questions Answered'. *The Hollywood Reporter*, 24 July 2011. http://www.hollywoodreporter.com/live-feed/comic-con-2011-meets-doctor-214778. Accessed 13 August 2016.

Nixon, Shaun, 'Is **Doctor Who** Science-Fiction or Fantasy?'. Overthinking It, 12 January 2016. https://www.overthinkingit.com/2016/01/12/is-doctor-who-science-fiction-or-fantasy. Accessed 13 August 2016.

Pape, Robert, 'Blowing Up an Assumption'. *New York Times*, 18 May 2005. http://www.nytimes.com/2005/05/18/opinion/blowing-up-an-assumption.html. Accessed 13 August 2016.

Risley, Matt, '**Doctor Who** *The God Complex*: Review'. IGN, 18 September 2011. http://uk.ign.com/articles/2011/09/18/doctor-who-the-god-complex-review. Accessed 13 August 2016.

Sandifer, Phil, 'A Great, Great Partnership (The God Complex)'. Eruditorum Press, 2014. http://www.eruditorumpress.com/blog/a-great-great-partnership-the-god-complex. Accessed 13 August 2016.

Sandifer, Phil, 'Q & A of the Damned'. Eruditorum Press, 2014. http://www.eruditorumpress.com/blog/qa-of-the-damned/. Accessed 13 August 2016.

Southall, JR, 'Interview: **Being Human** Showrunner Toby Whithouse'. *Starburst Magazine*, April 2012. http://www.starburstmagazine.com/features/feature-articles/2612-interview-toby-whithouse-being-human-doctor-who. Accessed 13 August 2016.

Waldman, Annie, 'Echo Chambers'. BBC News, 29 July 2014. http://www.bbc.co.uk/news/blogs-echochambers-28537149. Accessed 13 August 2016.

Witherington, Ben, 'Fear-Based Thinking Vs Faith-Based Thinking'. *Patheos*, 30 March 2015. http://www.patheos.com/blogs/bibleandculture/2015/03/30/fear-based-thinking-vs-faith-based-thinking/. Accessed 13 August 2016.

'Woodturtle', 'The **Doctor Who** Muslim Fail'. *Womanist Musings*, 2011. http://www.womanistmusings.com/doctor-who-muslim-fail/. Accessed 13 August 2016.

Ziolkowski, Theodore, 'Dürrenmatt's Fiction: Introduction'. University of Chicago Press. http://www.press.uchicago.edu/books/durrenmatt/vol2_introduction.html. Accessed 13 August 2016.

BIOGRAPHY

Paul Driscoll, an Oxford University postgraduate in theology, currently lives in Greater Manchester.

Paul has written of his love for **Doctor Who** and other classic British cult TV in the **You and Who** series of books, including *Contact Has Been Made*, *Blake's Heaven*, and *You and Who Else* (Watching Books).

His published short fiction includes 'Storage Wars' and 'The Time Lord Who Came to Tea', in the charity anthology, *Seasons of War* (Chinbeard Books), and the Iris Wildthyme adventure 'The Story Sorters', in *A Clockwork Iris* (Obverse Books).

He has also written about his experiences in setting up a homelessness charity in *Volunteering and Giving Back* (Chicken Soup for the Soul), and is currently working on his first novel, an alternative take on the origins of Christianity.